A Saga of Agony and Shame

Child Labour and Child Abuse in India
and the SAARC Countries

A Saga of Agony and Shame

Child Labour and Child Abuse in India and the SAARC Countries

M.S. Bhattacharya

Decent Books
New Delhi

Cataloging in Publication Data — DK
[Courtesy: D.K. Agencies (P) Ltd. <docinfo@dkagencies.com>]

Bhattacharya, M.S., 1956-
A saga of agony and shame : child labour and child abuse in India and the SAARC countries / M.S. Bhattacharya.
ix, 123 p., 23 cm.
Includes bibliographical references.
Includes index.
ISBN 8186921400

1. Child labor. India. 2. Child labor — South Asia. 3. Child abuse — India. 4. Child abuse — South Asia. 5. Juvenile justice. Administration of — India. 6. Juvenile justice. Administration of — South Asia. I. Titel.

ISBN 81-86921-40-0
First Published in India in 2007

Published by:
Decent Books
D-36/A-1, Mohan Garden
Najafgarh Road
New Delhi - 110 059
Ph. (011) 2535-3435

Distributed by:
D.K. Printworld (P) Ltd.
Regd. office : *'Sri Kunj,'* F-52, Bali Nagar
Ramesh Nagar Metro Station
New Delhi - 110 015
Phones : (011) 2545-3975, 2546-6019; *Fax* : (011) 2546-5926
E-mail : dkprintworld@vsnl.net
Web : www.dkprintworld.com

Printed by: D.K. Printworld (P) Ltd., New Delhi.

Dedicated to

Millions of hapless
Child Workers of South Asia

Preface

THIS book presents a study of child labour, child abuse and juvenile delinquency in India and the SAARC countries. As we will see in the pages that follow, a detailed discourse on any of these issues almost invariably involves the other two since they are inextricably linked with each other. Although child rights have become the focus of popular attention in recent times, little has been written on it so far, encompassing all its relevant aspects. Poverty, natural calamities, a hostile social milieu and conservative popular mindset are the basic reasons behind perpetuation of child labour and child abuse in India and other SAARC countries. I have given attention to all these factors instead of emphasizing poverty as the sole reason behind the problems.

Child rights, child labour and child abuse were phrases unknown in ancient and medieval world and in the eyes of law there was not much difference between an adult and a child offender. A delinquent juvenile was treated on a par with an adult criminal. Criminal jurisprudence took a long time to recognize child rights. In India significant steps have been taken in this direction through articles 24 and 45 of the Indian Constitution, *Child Labour Act, 1986, Care and Protection of Children Act, 2000, Juvenile Justice Act, 1986,* their subsequent amendments and similar other legislations. But in reality more often than not they are honoured in violation. Further, many Governmental agencies adopt a slapdash approach to the problem despite strictures from the courts of law. It seems common people are also not much aware of the magnitude of the problem. In eighteenth century Europe *enlightenment* had brought about a change in the attitude of the people to the problem of child abuse, and when in industries child labour became a commonplace there was widespread protest against it. In India both child labour and child abuse have assumed alarming proportions as we will see in this study; and eradication of poverty, change in social psyche, extensive welfare measures by the governmental and non-governmental agencies and stern action against the people who abuse children hold the key to solving the problem.

This work is based on contemporary newspapers and periodicals, official records and oral evidence collected from different Indian states. To collect evidence as well as photographs, I have extensively travelled to different regions of the subcontinent in 2004-05.

I am grateful to the National Library, Kolkata & Archives of some Indian states for the assistance I have received from them. I also owe a debt of gratitude to the members of my family for their constant co-operation during the preparation of this work.

August 15, 2006 **M.S. Bhattacharya**
Kolkata

Contents

Introduction

MANY people tend to think that the genesis of child labour should be traced back to the prehistoric times. Indeed children were often exposed to hard work even in the ancient world. The *Jataka* stories, the *Purana*s, the *Ramayana* and the *Mahabharata* provide us with numerous instances of children working hard for one reason or the other. A young student in ancient India strictly obeyed the order of his *guru*, performed the household chores at his preceptor's house[1] where agriculture and tending of cattle[2] possibly demanded his constant attention. But it would be difficult to find out sufficient evidence to suggest that Indian society was unkind to the young. Even slave children were not to be treated cruelly. Kautilya in his *Arthashastra* expressly mentions[3]:

> When a child is begotten on a female slave by her master, both the child and its mother shall at once be recognised as free. If for the sake of subsistence, the mother has to remain in her bondage, her brother and sister shall be liberated.

Such rules, it would possibly be argued, sought to condemn adultery; nevertheless it would be safe to hold that the lawmakers of ancient India were not unkind to the children. Even in the medieval period, child labour, as people conceive

---

1. *Vishnupurana*, Part III, Sec, ix, 1-7.
2. Ibid.
3. *Kautilya's Arthashastra* (tr. Dr. S. Shamasastry), p. 207, Mysore, 1929.

of today, was virtually non-existent. No doubt slave trade and employment of slave labour were rampant as fourteenth century Arab traveller Ibn Batuta witnessed during his stay in India.[4]

Batuta bought an exquisitely beautiful slave girl named Asura from a mart in Eastern India while his companion bought a boy slave named Lulu. Slave labour was cheap as we learn from the source. But neither in agriculture nor in trade and commerce it was employed on a large scale in medieval India. Agrarian economy had no demand for child labour to augment its production. At the most a child was employed as a part-time agricultural worker or a boy servant.

In fact employment of child workers on a large scale was an outcome of industrialization of which the genesis should be traced to the late eighteenth century Europe, particularly England. Starting from England, the industrial revolution had gradually transformed the society and economy of almost the whole of Europe. England, followed by Belgium, France and Germany witnessed the transformation well ahead of southern and eastern Europe. Many old towns and prosperous villages became depopulated as people rushed to the industrial towns in search of livelihood.[5] Epoch-making changes took place in almost every sphere of man's life:[6]

> The activities of the more progressive nations were diverted from agriculture to industry. The population was swept off the land and herded into towns. The hand-worker gave way to the machine; the workshop to the factory. . . The

---

4. See for details - R. Chakraborty, *Gourer Itihas* (ed. M.S. Bhattacharyya) pp. 195-96, Kolkata, 1999.
5. Arthur Birnie, *An Economic History of Europe,* p. 10, London. 1951.
6. Ibid., Introduction, p. VIII ff.

> older economic organization, with its small towns, its scattered industries, its local markets and its limited foreign trade, gave way to a system with densely populated industrial centres, large-scale production, world-wide trade and world division of labour.
>
> This economic revolution was accompanied by a social transformation. Since the middle ages, European society had been predominantly agrarian. The two important social classes were the landowners and the peasants; the landowners who performed the work of government, and the peasants who supplied their masters with the material necessities of life.
>
> . . .The growth of industrialism introduced disturbing elements into this social organization. It created new classes and upset the balance between the old. The importance of landowners and peasants declined; that of traders and industrialists steadily increased. Most significant of all, there emerged a new class, the industrial wage-earners or the proletariat, destined to be the storm-centre of the social welfare of the future.

Social changes were very much perceptible. Once settled in an industrial town, the wage-earners had a different life to lead. As the adults headed for the mills in the morning, the children were left uncared for, undernourished and ill-educated or illiterate. Eventually, hardship suffered by the family forced the children also to work in the mills which were 'dark, dingy and satanic' in the words of poet William Blake (1757-1827).

In India also many changes came about when industrialization started in the big towns like Kolkata, Mumbai and Chennai at a much later date[7] compared to Europe:

---

7. R. Ramachandran, *Urbanisation and Urban Systems in India*, p. 67, New Delhi, 1997.

> The industrial revolution that originated in England in the later half of the 18th century, took a full hundred years to reach India. The early factory industries to emerge in India were the cotton textile industry in Bombay and Ahmedabad, jute in Calcutta and coal mining in the Damodar Basin. There was some scattered development of the cotton textile industry in other parts of India as well. Kanpur and Jamshedpur were the only truly industrial cities to emerge during the British rule; Kanpur specialized in the leather and woolen textile industries, while Jamshedpur, established in 1907, was the main iron and steel centre in India until 1947. Industrial development in India before independence was indeed very modest. Most industries were located in existing towns, principally the colonial metropolitan cities of Bombay, Calcutta and Madras. Calcutta and Bombay were the only cities in which distinct industrial areas developed.

Necessity of large-scale production initiated thousands of children into the industries. The most painful aspect of child labour in these modern industries was the treatment meted out to the young workers. They were as a rule niggardly paid.[8] Moreover, rural society didn't deprive a child of parental and family care even when he was exposed to hard labour as an agricultural worker. The peasantry and the tribal societies took care of their children as part of their culture. But in an industrial town, the child workers remained helpless until political and social movements sought to better their condition.[9] Such movements were actually initiated in the early twentieth century.

---

8. Dewan Chamanlal, *Coolie — The story of Labour and Capital in India*, vol. II, p. 18.

9. See for details, R.D. Das, *Factory Labour in India*, Berlin, 1923.

The second half of the nineteenth century witnessed the ever- expanding procession of child workers entering into the mills of Kolkata and Mumbai, the plantations of Assam and Bengal, the railroad construction projects almost throughout the length and breadth of the country and the ports, marts and commercial hubs in search of livelihood. We should not fail to note in this connection that industrialization in the late nineteenth century and early twentieth century India was far from revolution as she remained predominantly agrarian with an urban population of 8.7 per cent as late as 1872 which rose to 11 per cent at the turn of the century.[10] Nevertheless, industrialization had its far-reaching effects on the society. There began a rush to the big towns particularly from their neighbouring regions and immediate vicinity. Ahmedabad and Mumbai had their supply of labour from the Gujarat villages and the Ratnagiri district in Konkan. Another concrete example was that of the jute mills of Kolkata where a majority of workers came from the neighbouring states of U.P, Orissa and Bihar. The tea plantations of Assam and Bengal were exceptions as their workers had their roots in distant Central India wherefrom labour contractors brought them to the plantation areas.[11] Such migration and displacement immensely contributed to the problem of child labour.

Irrespective of his place of work the child worker suffered miserably. In colonial India, child labour became indispensable to almost all factories engaged in large-scale production. The niggardly-paid child worker was deprived of nourishment, healthcare and education. In Europe things improved with

---

10. R. Ramachandran, Ibid. p. 61 ff.
11. See for details — D. Ganguli, *Slavery in British Dominions,* (ed. S. Kundu) Introduction, p. 5. New Edition, Kolkata, 1972.

the passage of time.[12] But in India and other third world countries appreciable changes are yet to come. Millions of child workers still toil in the modern industrial units, agricultural fields, farm houses, *mandis* of the big towns, lanes and by-lanes of the Indian cities specializing in furniture, electronic gadgets, hand-made cheroots, carpets, plastic goods, book binding, shoe manufacturing, explosive fire works and so on. As the young child worker grows up, he loses his job since his employer never agrees to pay him better wages. Once he loses his job, he turns into a delinquent joining the gangs of muggers, pick-pockets and other lawbreakers. Once punished for an offence his chances of rehabilitation become remote in the true sense of the term. As a recent report from Mumbai revealed:[13]

> After spending three years in an observation house for having committed a robbery, the day of his release should have been the happiest in 18 year old Sanju's life. But with no family to go home to and no training to get him a job, Sanju, like other children in conflict with the law, was suddenly left into no future the day he turned 18.
>
> The *Juvenile Justice Act*, though hailed by child rights activists as progressive and undoubtedly child-friendly, is seeing very poor implementation everywhere and especially in Mumbai, where large number of street children need special attention.

Rehabilitation of rescued children has always remained a problem. It's more acute in the case of children of foreign countries rescued from Indian territory. Time and again in this dissertation, we have discussed the plight of the children of the neighbouring countries caught in the trap of traffickers.

---

12. Arthur Birnie, Ibid., pp. 188 ff.
13. *The Times of India*, Kolkata, October 12, 2004.

Community Puja-Pandal highlighting child labour.
South Kolkata, October 2004. (Courtesy: Shinjini Bhattacharya)

Sculpted figure of a child worker with tears rolling down his face.
Figure of a boy cobbler forms the spire of the pandal.
A view of a Kolkata Puja-Pandal, October 2004.

Depiction of a boy brick layer carrying brick,
Pandal decoration at South Kolkata, October 2004.
(Courtesy: Sayantani Bhattacharya)

In a recent incident, the plight of a group of Bangladeshi children trapped in Kolkata became the focus of popular attention. They were altogether fourteen in number; aged between five and twelve years. A volunteer of Bangladesh Women Lawyers Forum visited Kolkata to escort the children home. Red-tapism and unwillingness of the BSF and the BDR inordinately delayed the process of their journey home.[14] Meanwhile, a child named Munna, aged 10, one of the fourteen hapless boys, died in Kolkata and Sayeeda Sabeha, the Bangladeshi lawyer left for home since her visa had expired. The children were destined to suffer many more days of confinement in the shelters in West Bengal provided by the government. Their deportation at an early date depended on the NGOs engaged in child welfare activities. In most cases, they alone look after the rescued children. But in spite of their best efforts, as we have seen, it becomes difficult to send them back expeditiously. The rescued children are produced before the Juvenile court. They are usually kept in recognized "rescue homes" or shelters. A good deal of communications meanwhile, initiate the process of deportation. Such deportations are to be mutually agreed upon by the concerned governments. At long last comes the question of satisfying the paramilitary forces manning the international borders. In the case under discussion the last hurdle proved to be insurmountable.[15]

Yet another important aspect of child labour is that the child workers in most cases are cut off from their roots. It is the co-worker who befriends a child worker. But when a child worker changes his place of work he suffers from alienation which affects his psyche. This eventually can lead him to the world of crime.

---

14. *The Anandabazar Patrika,* Kolkata, October 13, 2004.
15. Ibid.

Far worse is the condition of an ailing child worker. There's none to look after a sick boy or girl because of isolation from society and family. As a leading Kolkata daily has reported:[16]

> Malati Das was only 16 when she was dumped in Medical College and Hospital by her employers. Five years later, she was carried out in a stretcher, dead.
>
> Malati died at 9.45 A.M. on Friday. It was not pulmonary tuberculosis alone that killed her, loneliness is an equally painful sore. Her employers, who live a few metres away on College Street, never came to visit her in these five years. Nor did her family in South 24 Parganas. No one even came to claim her body; it was handed over to police by the hospital authorities.

Almost everywhere in India one would come across the hapless child workers bearing the burden of civilization. But article 24 of the Constitution of India clearly states that no child below the age of fourteen years shall be employed to work in any factory or mine or engaged in any hazardous work. Many years elapsed since the promulgation of the Constitution in 1950. But appreciable changes are yet to come. Nevertheless, every cloud has a silver lining. The apex court of India in a judgement dated 10.12.1996 has ordered for elimination of child labour. Moreover there is a rising consciousness among the people of India about the baneful effects of child labour on society. Several NGOs have in fact given a fillip to the growing movement against child labour. The issue, as we all know has already been internationalized. A recent conference[17] held in Hyderabad was of considerable importance. Organizations working for the rehabilitation of

---

16. *The Times of India*, Kolkata, November 6, 2004.
17. *Deccan Chronicle*, Hyderabad, November 2, 2004.

child labour in 20 developing and underdeveloped countries met in the city. Such meetings were unheard of, a generation earlier. Interestingly, public feeling about child labour was evident when in October 2004, a community Durga Puja *pandal* in South Kolkata was decorated with sculptures of varieties of child workers with a large sculpted figure of a shoe-shine boy forming the spire of the makeshift temple. It amazed the viewers and they didn't fail to appreciate the enthusiasm. Doubtless in recent years public attitude in India towards child abuse has shifted to a certain degree in the positive direction. In the neighbouring countries also the recent wave of enthusiasm in this regard is worthy of appreciation. A Nepalese film on child abuse and trafficking in young girls, namely *Mo Kashari Bhanu* (How do I say) shot in Nepal, Manipur, Nagaland and West Bengal has generated much enthusiasm. A movement has also been launched against child abuse[18] in Nepal.

In Pakistan, human rights activists have launched a campaign against the football manufacturers who employ thousands of underprivileged children.[19]

It is indeed popular resistance that can put an end to child labour and we have to pin our hopes on the changing mindset of the people about it.

---

18. *The Times of India*, January 19, 2006.
19. *The Anandabazar Patrika*, June 23, 2006.

1

Child Labour in Colonial India

INDUSTRIALISATION had a shattering effect on the lives of thousands of children in Europe. In Asia also the children employed as workers suffered a similar fate some time later. In fact each child worker on earth is a David Copperfield.

> . . . I became, at ten years old a little labouring mind in the service of Murdstone and Grinby. . .
>
> . . . Murdstone and Grinby's trade was among a good many kinds of people, but an important branch of it was the supply of wines and spirits to certain packet-ships. I forget now where they chiefly went, but I think there were some among them that made voyages both to the East and West Indies. I know that a great many empty bottles were one of the consequences of this traffic, and that certain men and boys were employed to examine them against the light, and reject those that were flawed, and to rinse and wash them. When the empty bottles ran short, there were labels to be pasted on full ones, or corks to be fitted to them, or seals to be put upon the corks, or finished bottles to be packed in casks. All this work was my work, and of boys employed upon it I was one.
>
> . . . No words can express the secret agony of my soul as I sunk into this companionship; compared these henceforth everyday associates with those of my happier childhood — not to say with Steerforth, Traddles, and the rest of those

> boys; and felt my hopes of growing up to be a learned and distinguished man, crushed in my bosom. The deep remembrance of the sense I had, of being utterly without hope now; of the shame I felt in my position; of the misery it was to my young heart to believe that day by day what I had learned, and thought, and delighted in, and raised my fancy and my emulation up by, would pass away from me, little by little, never to be brought back any more; cannot be written. As often as Mick Walker went away in the course of that forenoon, I mingled my tears with the water in which I was washing the bottles; and sobbed as if there were a flow in my own breast, and it were in danger of bursting.
>
> — David Copperfield

Nowhere in world literature possibly we come across a delineation of the agonies of a child labourer that can surpass in sensitivity the above statement. Charles Dickens, a nineteenth century man himself, could feel the pang a child worker was exposed to in the post-industrial revolution England. Things gradually improved in England, Belgium, France, Germany, and other industrial societies in Europe through social and political movements and consequent labour legislations.[1] But in the Afro-Asian countries where industrialization took place much later, things remained the same even in the early years of the new millennium. In the Indian subcontinent, colonial administration was not favourably disposed to the idea of legislation that could mitigate the sufferings of the labourers as well as child workers.

In colonial India, bonded or indentured labour formed part and parcel of the industrial establishment. Dewan

1. See for details - Arthur Birnie, *An Economic History of Europe* 1760-1939 pp. 118 ff. In the words of Birnie, "In every European country the rise of a class of industrial workers has been followed at longer or shorter intervals by a labour movement, an organized attempt of the wage-earners to improve their standard of life."

Chamanlal, a twentieth century author and social activist offers a curious description of how children, as young as five, were employed in a carpet factory in the city of Amritsar in the Punjab, owned by an Anglo-Greek business house. A ledger discovered from the factory revealed a sordid story of exploitation. A certain Buta of Amritsar had borrowed Rs. 57 from the owners of the factory and two of his grandsons were held in debt bondage by the lenders as securtiy. The two young boys received Rs. 9 and Rs. 7 respectively as monthly wages.[2] The incident took place in the early part of the twentieth century. It would be safe to presume that the situation was more or less the same in the earlier period. The factory owners, planters and traders enjoyed legal protection under certain Acts like, the *Masters and Servants Act, The Workmen's Breach of Contract Act, Assam Plantation Labour Immigration Act, Madras Planter's Labour Act* etc. This set of laws aimed at restraining the rights of the labourers, provided for severe punishment in cases where a labourer escaped from his place of work to avoid brutal treatment, or disagreed to obey the commands of his employer. Sections 490 and 492 of the Indian Penal Code, introduced in 1860, also provided for punishment in such cases. The *Employers and Workers (Disputes) Act,* purportedly labour friendly, contained provisions for penalty and imprisonment of a worker in case of failure to carry out the orders of his or her employer.[3]

The industrial and agricultural workers in post-mutiny India directly under the British rule were in a desperate plight as wages were low, price level was soaring up and the entire working class population was virtually unorganized. Mid nineteenth century India had three large presidency towns,

2. Chamanlal Dewan, *Coolie : The Story of Labour and Capital in India,* vol. I, p.16.
3. S. Sen, *Bharter Sramik Andolaner Itihas,* vol. I, p. 81, Kolkata, 1984.

namely Calcutta, Bombay and Madras, known as the big hubs of trade and Industry. Politically and commercially Calcutta was the premier city as the seat of the British Indian Government and the largest centre of industrial activities. Even in Bengal presidency with its largest industrial establishment, workers were niggardly paid. The public works department paid 7 paise to 13 paise on an average in 1867-68. Obviously 7 paise was meant for a child worker while 13 paise was the wage received by an adult skilled worker. The daily wages paid in Bombay were 37 paise, 25 paise and 18 paise respectively to a male, female and child worker in the same period. In the Punjab, the rate varied between 12 paise and 30 paise per day. In the central provinces the rate was 18 paise on an average.[4] The rate was particularly low in Bengal possibly because of its huge and populous North Indian hinterland which could supply more labour than the market actually demanded.

It will possibly be more interesting to go into details taking into consideration varieties of labour and their respective rates beyond the purview of the public works department. Let's now turn to a district far away from the metropolis.

The Annual General Administration Report of Bhagalpur Division (situated in Bihar) offers some curious information. The prices of labour in the district of Malda which formed part of the division between 1876 and 1906 are given in table I on page 14:[5]

No deliberation about wage and labour would be adequate without a reference to the price level of the material period.

4. G. Kaushal, *Economic History of India*, 1757-1966, p. 343, New Delhi, 1991.

5. *Annual General Administration Report, Bhagulpore Division*: 1895-96, progs. of the Lt. Governor of Bengal, December 1896.

Table - I

Wages received during different years

Type of labour	**1893-94**			**1894-95**			**1895-96**		
	Rupee	**Anna**	**Pai**	**Rupee**	**Anna**	**Pai**	**Rupee**	**Anna**	**Pai**
Mason	0	8	0	0	8	0	0	8	0
Common Mason	0	5	0	0	5	0	0	5	0
Superior Carpenter	0	8	0	0	8	0	0	8	5
Common Carpenter	0	5	0	0	5	0	0	5	0
Coolie	0	3	0	0	3	0	0	3	0
Woman	0	2	0	0	2	0	0	2	0
Boy	0	1	6	0	1	6	0	1	6
Gharami (Hut builder)	0	5	0	0	5	0	0	4	3
Superior Blacksmith	0	8	0	0	8	0	0	8	0
Common Blacksmith	0	5	0	0	5	0	0	5	0

Table II offers information about the price level prevalent in the district.[6]

Table - II

Year	Qty. of Common Rice (Per Re.) *Seer-Chhatak*	Qty. of Wheat (Per Re.) *Seer-Chhatak*	Qty. of Gram (Per Re.) *Seer-Chhatak*	Qty. of Salt (Per Re.) *Seer-Chhatak*
1893-94	15-0	16-0	16-0	10-0
1894-95	16-12	12-4	15-0	19-0
1895-96	16-0	13-4	18-2	10-0

Therefore, a boy worker would be able to buy a little more than a seer[7] of rice with his average daily wage.

G.E. Lambourn, writing in 1918, gives an account of price level for more than half a century in the district.[8]

Table - III

	1853-54 Qty. per Re.	1870 Qty. per Re.	1890 Qty. per Re.	1910 Qty. per Re.
Common rice	37-69	30-06	15-74	13-58
Wheat	40-00	21-26	17-74	11-25
Maize	74-12	40-00	N.A.	26-35

The figures represent mainly export price at the river marts as Lambourn informs us:[9]

> In 1888 a detailed economic enquiry was made in some of the villages of the district.[10] It was found that for agricultural

6. Ibid.
7. Seer: Indian denomination of weight usually a little less than a kilogram.
8. G.E. Lambourn, *Bengal District Gazetteers, Malda*, pp. 53 ff., Kolkata, 1918.
9. Ibid.
10. Ibid., pp. 55-56.

> labourers the average wage per day was 2 *annas* for men, and for boys one *anna*, with two meals of the value of 9 *pies* and 6 *pies*, respectively, while for harvesting one sixth of the grain was given to the reaper.
>
> For the servants engaged by the year the rates were Rs. 21 for men and Rs. 9 for boys, with food to the value of Rs. 24/- and Rs. 18/- and clothes to the value of Rs. 2-4 and Rs. 1-5, respectively.

So the adult and the child both led a miserable life. Their condition drifted from bad to worse with the passage of time.

A very important aspect of Bengal's economy was tea plantation of the northern districts of Darjeeling and Jalpaiguri. Tea plantation in Darjeeling[11] was initiated in 1856 while in Jalpaiguri it was introduced[12] as late as 1874. As we do not have sufficient information about child labour in tea gardens in the nineteenth century we are largely dependent on J.F. Gruning's account for the early years of the twentieth century.[13]

The average monthly earnings of labourers engaged in tea plantation were in 1911 Rs. 6/- for men, Rs. 4.50 to Rs. 5/- for women and Rs. 2.50 to Rs. 3/- for children. L.S.S.O'-malley gives almost identical figures[14] for Darjeeling plantation labourers. Adult males Rs. 6/-, adult females Rs. 4.50 and

---

11. A.K. Banerjee, et al., *West Bengal District Gazetteers, Darjeeling*, p. 99, Kolkata, 1980.
12. A.M. Kushari, et al., *West Bengal District Gazetteers, Jalpaiguri*, p. 130, Kolkata, 1981.
13. J.F. Gruning, *Eastern Bengal and Assam District Gazetteers, Jalpaiguri*, p. 96, Allahabad, 1911.
14. L.S.S. O 'Malley, *Bengal District Gazetteers, Darjeeling*, p. 111, Kolkata, 1907.

children Rs. 3/-. Once again we have to compare the wage earned by the plantation workers with the price level.[15]

The average price for common rice for the period 1893-1902 was about Rs. 3/- a maund (100 bbs or 40 kgs). There was little change in the next three years, but in 1906 the price rose to about Rs. 4.50/- a maund and in 1908 to Rs. 5/- a maund. By 1912 the price came down again and varied between Rs. 3.25 and 3.81 a maund in January and September respectively. For the next three years the price rise was continuous and reached the height of Rs. 6.66 a maund in 1915.

So the boy workers in the Tea gardens received starvation wages almost throughout the British period. They were unable to fend for themselves unless supported by their parents. The orphans were in fact the most unfortunate lot.

Let us now look into the condition of the children in the Assam tea gardens in the nineteenth century. A Kolkata newspaper provides horrifying information.[16]

> When adult life in tea-gardens is exposed to considerable risk and when there is frightful mortality among adult labourers, it is no wonder that child life, which always requires very tender care and nursing should be exposed to even greater risks. We thus find that in 1884 the death rate among the children in tea-gardens had risen from 39.7 to 44 per thousand. While the death rate has gradually fallen, in 1882, it was 39.7 per thousand, in 1883 it was 34.3 and in 1884 it further decreased to 32.2 per thousand.

The newspaper also quoted the statement of the civil surgeon of Dibrugarh, a district which had vast tea plantations within its area:[17]

---

15. J.F. Grunning, Ibid., p. 97.
16. *The Bengalee*, October 30, 1886.
17. *The Bengalee*, November 6, 1886.

> The conditions of child life on a tea garden are altogether so unfavourable that the wonder is how so many children succeed in passing childhood's stage. A coolie woman gets a variable amount of leave for her confinement. After that, if the infant is not strangled at birth, she must either take it out to her work or leave it behind, with no one to look after it. In the former cases, tied to its mother's back or left in the nearest drain, it is exposed to extremes of heat and cold, to wind and to rain; in the latter the child gets half starved and so paves its way to a death from some bowel disorder or succeeds in cutting short its career by a fall or a roll into the open fire. So alive are coolie women to these facts that to avoid the trouble of bringing up their children under such circumstances, abortion is frequently resorted to, and *dais* who produce it often make their business a very profitable one.

The condition of the children within the tea estates remained unchanged until the *Plantation Labour Act* was passed in 1951 imposing certain restrictions on child labour.

A delegation of the British Trade Union Congress visiting India in 1928 had observed:[18]

> All enquires go to show that vast majority of workers in India do not receive more than about 1s per day. In the province of Bengal, which includes the largest mass of industrial workers, investigators declared that as far as they could ascertain, 60% of workers were in receipt of wages of not more than Is 2d. a day in the highest instance, scaling down to as low as 7d. to 9d. for men and 3d. to 7d. in the case of children and women. . . our enquiries support these figures and as a matter of fact many cases have been quoted to us of daily rates in operation which descend to 3 1/4 d. for women and 7d. or even less for men.

18. See for details — Sen, *Bharater Sramik Andolaner Itihas,* vol. II, p. 77.

The report of the delegation also revealed that industrial workers in India even in the largest city of Kolkata and the province of Bengal lived in abject poverty. The workers virtually received no education and their children were destined to suffer from malnutrition and myriad other aliments resulting from it.[19]

Furthermore, rural indebtedness was one of the principal reasons behind the ever-increasing flow of child labour to the industries in colonial India. By 1933, the debt in colonial India (exclusive of the princely states) was no less than 1200 crores.[20] This was unique to India. Authorities have attributed it to fragmented land holdings, low productivity of land often caused by vagaries of monsoon and even lack of skill and industry on the part of the farmers.[21] No doubt the reasons can be controverted. But the hardship caused by rural indebtedness and its relation with child labour in colonial India is undeniable.

Movements Against Child Labour and Labour Legislation in Colonial India

The Movement against child labour in India was actually initiated by Sorabjee Sapurjee Bengalee. His basic intention was to reduce the working hours of a child worker and increase his wages. Since his petitions to Bombay Government produced no results he corresponded with John Croft of Manchester to enlist his support to his movement. In fact niggardly paid child

---

19. Ibid.
20. P.J. Thomas, *The Problem of Rural Indebtedness,* p. 19.
21. See for details — G. Kaushal, *Economic History of India,* 1757-1966, pp. 179 ff, New Delhi, 1991; For a detailed discussion of the competition between Bombay and Manchester see, Edward C. Moulton, *Lord Northbrook's Indian Administration* 1872-76, pp. 185 ff., Mumbai, 1968, S. Sen, op. cit., vol. I, p. 81, Kolkata, 1984.

workers were to be credited for the low cost of production in Indian factories which directly hampered the interest of British industries. So the cloth manufacturers of Manchester demanded certain regulations to restrict female and child labour in India.[21] There was a hue and cry in England against exploitation of workers in India and the poor wages they were offered. The issue was raised in the House of Commons and the intervention of the Secretary of State for India was sought. Consequently the Bombay Government appointed a nine-member commission of which seven represented the industrialists of Bombay. The report of the commission, as was expected, made no recommendation for the betterment of the condition of Indian workers.[22] Eventually the *Indian Factories Act* was passed in 1881 which prohibited the employment of children below seven years of age in Indian factories and the working hours for children between seven and twelve years were restricted to nine hours a day only.[23]

The *Factory Act* also provided for one hour's daily rest during working hours and four holidays every month. Restrictions were also imposed on the employment of women and children at night.[22] Interestingly, educated Indian gentry, obsessed with nationalist sentiments, criticised the *Factory Act* as an imperialist ploy to destroy the fledgling Bombay industries. Historian Sumit Sarkar observes:[24]

> Nationalist opinion also usually refused to concern itself with the plight of Indians working in Indian-owned factories, in sharp contrast to those employed by foreigners, for whom (as for the Assam Coolies) humanitarian sentiments were often expressed. The Factory Act, which put certain minimal and ill-enforced restrictions on the employment of women

22. Ibid., p. 82.
23. Ibid.
24. Ibid., pp. 78 ff.

> and children and which the Government passed mainly at the instance of a Lancashire worried by Bombay competition, were opposed by most nationalist newspapers. Only an overriding concern for the future of India's cotton textile industry can explain (though not excuse) the callous brutality of statements like that of the *Amritabazar Patrika* of 2nd September, 1875: "A larger death-rate amongst our operatives is far more preferable to the collapse of this rising industry."

In the late forties of the twentieth century trade union movements in the tea plantations gained some momentum. The leaders of the movement now paid some attention to the hardship of the child workers. *The Darjeeling District Chiya Kaman Majdoor Union* served a charter of demands to the management which included the following:[25]

> Adult male workers should get 1 Rupee for 10 lbs. of leaf and 1 *Anna* for each extra pound. Adult female workers should get 12 *Anna*s and boy and girl workers 9 *Anna*s and 6 *Anna*s respectively. These minimum wages should remain constant throughout the year.

The charter of demand discriminated against the children, particularly the girls. Where demands themselves were irrational their fulfilment would effect little change. So the condition of child workers in the tea estates remained almost the same till 1947.

Not much better was the condition of child workers elsewhere. In the Moghul Gardens of the viceregal palace of New Delhi as many as fifty children were engaged to scare away the birds even during the last days of the Raj.[26]

---

25. Sumit Sarkar, *Modern India*, 1885-1947, p. 87, New Delhi, 1984.
26. Larry Collins and Dominique Lapierre, *Freedom at Midnight*, pp. 118 ff., New Delhi, 1976.

2

The Forms of Child Labour and the Plight of the Child Workers in South Asia

PREVALENCE of a myriad of forms of child labour in the third world including India boggles our mind. In respect of forms of child labour in India most valuable information is provided by the census of India 1981.[1] It has classified child labour in nine industrial divisions. These are: 1. Cultivation 2. Agricultural labour 3. Livestock, Forestry, Fishing, Plantation 4. Mining and Quarrying 5. Manufacturing, Processing, Servicing and Repairs 6. Construction 7. Trade and Commerce 8. Transport, Storage and Communication 9. Other services. We learn from the same source that the majority of rural child workers (84.29%) are engaged in cultivation and agricultural labour while manufacturing, processing, servicing and repairs are the fields which employ the majority of child workers in urban areas. But from the above classification we do not get a real life-picture of the numerous varieties of child labour in India.

Manufacturers of brassware, hand-knitted wool carpets, explosive fire works, footwear, hand-blown glass bangles, hand-made locks, hand dipped matches, hand-broken quarried stones, hand-spun silk thread, hand-loomed silk cloth; hand-

---

1. Census of India 1981.

made bricks and *bidis* (hand-made Indian cherrots) employ forced or indentured child labour in India.[2]

Bonded Labour and Traffic in Children

We have come across some horrifying information about bonded child labour and slavery from certain sources. In the annual cattle fair of Sonepur in Bihar, children are sold like cattle by the racketeers.[3] Selling young boys and girls into slavery is not really unusual in India. A leading Indian daily has recently reported:[4]

> In the face of abject poverty, a scheduled caste woman from Gajipur has sold off her infant son for Rs. 6000. And this was the third such incident in the past four months in this state (Bihar).
>
> Bhirana Devi, wife of rickshaw puller Lalbabu Paswan, was finding it increasingly difficult to bring up her two month old son. She had lost a child owing to the absence of proper medical facilities only two months back. This time, she took no chances, especially when the child fell sick for a few days. And apparently, to save the child both from possible death and poverty, she sold him off to a person from the nearby Patori village for Rs. 6000.
>
> Only in June, a poverty-stricken minority-caste family, from Haji Harmain Nagar in Patna's Fulwarisharif block, had "handed over" its newborn son to a neighbour to ensure a better upbringing for him. The couple — Md. Bhatt and his wife Nujahat — gave the child to one Md. Kalam, a resident

---

2. See for details — Country Reports on Human Rights Practices — 1999 February 25, 2000.
3. Ibid.
4. *The Statesman*, Kolkata, September 14, 2004.

> of Isapur Naharpura, as they realized it was beyond them to rise the child "properly."
>
> The same month another destitute minority-caste [*sic*] family, residing in the same Fulwari Sharif area, was forced to "part with" its newborn baby again for the child's "proper care." The couple — Md. Suhail and Gudia — from Isapur has handed over their six-day old boy to a local policeman.

Traffic in children has been reported from Orissa also. The district of Kalahandi in Orissa has experienced worst droughts in recent years leading to catastrophic losses as is well-known. The socio-economic effects of such disasters are appalling:[5]

> Bhawanipatna Oct. 15 — Kusum Majhi a tribal of Pastipada village allegedly sold her 20-day old baby girl to a rickshaw puller, Dhanu Naik, for Rs. 600. The incident took place at the district headquarters of Kalahandi. The girl was her second child, the first being a four-year old son. Kusum is said to have ignored attempts by a few people who implored her not to sell the child. She allegedly brought the excuse of social problems. In fact an agreement was signed in the presence of witnesses and the child was handed over.

Signing an agreement before selling a child is a very curious aspect of the incident. Possibly the practice of selling children is rampant in the region. Signing agreement for an illegal act is an underworld practice. We have reasons to believe that sale and abduction of children, plotted and executed by the criminal underworld, maintain steady supply of children to the labour market of India. Abduction of a 10-month old baby from a Kolkata slum and subsequent attempt to sell him to customers in an Arab state who conduct camel races, had

5. *The Statesman*, Kolkata, October 16, 2004.

recently been revealed. The child was abducted by a neighbour who sold him to agents who worked on behalf of customers in the Middle-East.[6]

It is worthwhile to mention that in the state of West Bengal illegal Bangladeshi immigrants were handled by racketeers for decades who sold them as bonded labourers. We have learnt from a human rights activist that such immigrants borrow money from the racketeers to pay for their passage to India through the international border, and work hard as bonded labourers in subsequent years to pay off their debts and buy freedom.[7] Many Indian and Bangladeshi boys, as *Country Reports on Human Rights Practices 1999* of the U.S. Dept. of State tells us, end up as riders in camel races in the Middle-East, especially in the United Arab Emirates. Some of the child riders, as young as four, earn their livelihood from the cruel medieval sport.[8]

A report of the *UN Working Group Report on Contemporary Forms of Slavery* mentioned the existence of a large number of bonded children working in four industries namely, silk weaving, flower growing, silver work and rolling *bidis*.[9]

Public opinion was stirred in June 2004 when 17 children were rescued from an embroidery factory in the city of Delhi

---

6. *The Anandabazar Patrika*, July 6, 2004.
7. See for details — Robert I. Friedman, "India's Shame : Sexual Slavery and Political Corruption are leading to an AIDS Catastrophe," (Art. in) *The Nation*, April 8, 1996; Interview with Mr B. Dutta, February 11, 2003 at Karimpur, Nadia (W.B.).
8. *Country Report on Human Rights Practices 1999*, U.S. Dept. of State, February 25, 2000.
9. "India Court Investigation Reveal Scale of Bonded Labour," *UN Working Group Report on Contemporary Forms of Slavery*, June 1996.

by *Bachpan Bachao Andolan* (BBA)[10] with the assistance of the State Labour Department. All these children belonged to the district of Purnea in Bihar. They were brought to Delhi from their villages by some relatives and labour recruiters sometime back. Three of them, Mohammed Haider, Nishat and Sahil were only nine years old while the eldest boy of the group namely Ranjeet was only 14. The boys were forced to work for more than 12 hours a day usually and when there was an increased demand of the clothes they embroidered, the hapless boys had to work for the whole night. They worked, cooked, washed and slept in the same room. A tubewell provided them water. Throughout the day, they were under the control and supervision of a manager who left for home every night locking their room from outside. The children lived in abject misery until they were rescued by the BBA.[11] We have more examples of such bonded labour from other parts of India as well.

In Kestopur near Kolkata a 12-year old girl who worked as a domestic help was rescued by her neighbours in October 2004. She suffered brutal tortures at the hands of her employer.[12]

The state of Andhra Pradesh in Southern India is infamous for being the largest supplier of children to the labour market[13]

---

10. BBA is a Delhi based NGO.
11. The incident caused sensation as several newspapers of Delhi published it in June 2004.
12. *The Anandabazar Patrika,* October 4, 2004.
13. According to a recent estimate, about 1.8 lakh children below 14 work illegally in the fields, factories, shops and restaurants in Andhra Pradesh alone — See for details. *The Telegraph,* May 24, 2005.

of India and the brothels of Dubai and other Gulf states.[14] The child workers in the southern cities of Chennai, Hyderabad and Bangalore are mostly from the backward districts of Tamilnadu, Andhra Pradesh and Karnataka. Many such children are held in debt bondage as is evident from the sources we have mentioned so far.

There are elements of bonded labour in *bidi* (small handmade Indian cheroot) industry also. Thousands of young boys and girls are employed in manufacturing *bidi*. In some cases parents or guardians of young children receive advance form the employer and in return deliver a stipulated quantity of finished goods. The contract often includes supply of tobacco and *Kendu* leaves with which the *bidi*s are rolled. The contractee employs all members of his family including the children to roll *bidi*s with the tobacco supplied by the employer. If he fails to deliver the goods within the stipulated time, a breach of contract takes place and the contractor dictates fresh terms to the disadvantage of the worker. The manufacturers also directly recruit labourers on fixed wages. The wage is determined by the quantity of *bidi*s rolled. Usually Rs.25 to Rs.30 is paid to the worker per thousand *bidi*s rolled. In the rural areas the rate is even lower depending on the supply of labour. Incidentally *bidi* manufacturing units have mushroomed in the most underdeveloped districts of West Bengal like Murshidabad and South 24 Parganas where labour is cheap. The average daily income of a child *bidi* worker does not exceed Rs. 45. Some interesting features of this industry are worth mentioning. A girl child in the regions we have

---

14. *The Statesman*, September 13, 2004. Extreme poverty in the rural districts of Andhra is the reason behind this. Farming has become unprofitable in recent times — See for details — S. Choudhury "Till Death do us Apart" (Art. in) *Outlook* June 7, 2004.

mentioned is often induced to learn the art of *bidi* rolling so that she can be a good marriage prospect. A boy worker tends to change his professions as he grows up but a girl, skilled in *bidi* rolling, seldom changes her profession in a conservative society and continues to supplement the low income of her family.

The largest *bidi* manufacturing units can be found in the Murshidabad district of West Bengal. Aurangabad, Dhulian, Farakka and Jangipur are among the towns in the district where the industry has flourished in recent times. Kaliachak (Malda dist., WB), Ranaghat (Nadia dist. WB), Jainagar (South 24 Parganas dist. WB), Buniadpur (South Dinajpur dist., W.B.), Baleswar (Baleswar dist., Orissa), Araria (Purnea dist., Bihar), Kishanganj (Kishanganj dist., Bihar), Dumka (Dumka dist. Jharkhand) have numerous large and small *bidi* manufacturing units. In each district mentioned heretofore thousands of *bidi* rolling children can be spotted under the road side shades, private houses, and the large buildings owned by manufacturers.[15]

The child workers employed in rolling *bidi* are either school drop-outs or illiterates. They are prone to pulmonary diseases like bronchitis and tuberculosis and other ailments, namely anaemia, dyspepsia, and muscular dystrophy. Pulmonary diseases and dyspepsia are attributable to handling of tobacco for a long time everyday, sometimes more than twelve or thirteen hours while muscular problems are caused by their sitting in the same posture, usually with legs placed one upon other, for a long time from early childhood. Their condition is much worse than the agricultural workers; nevertheless

15. Our survey about the *bidi*-rolling children was confined to Eastern India.

many of them have parents engaged in agriculture and the combined family income keeps the households afloat.[16]

The prevalence of bonded labour in Pakistan is no less shocking either where 3500-odd football manufacturers, mostly based in Sialkot, employ numerous children. The bangle industries of Hyderbad, the fishing ports of Baluchistan and the carpet and leather goods manufacturers, based in various provinces, also thrive on bonded labour.[17]

The Urchins and the Casual Workers

In a recent survey[18] we chanced to talk to 50 boys in Kolkata all of whom were from Orissa, Bihar, Jharkhand, Eastern U.P. and the rural districts of West Bengal and employed as ragpickers, shoe shine boys, tea stall workers, waiters in roadside restaurants and workers in repair shops for motor vehicles, garages and transport depots. About twenty of them had also worked as domestic helps earlier, earning Rs. 50/- to Rs. 100/- per month. Twice a day they were offered left overs or stale or rotten food as principal meal. They slept on floors of store rooms, kitchens and garages and were beaten up mercilessly for their failure to perform any work to the satisfaction of their employers. They had to do the cleaning, wash clothes and kitchen utensils and other household chores. All of them had to flee their employers' homes. Subsequently

---

16. *Gramonnayan Milan Samity* of Jaynagar (South 24 Parganas Dist., West Bengal), an NGO, has provided information about the *bidi* rolling children of the region.
17. See for details *The Anandabazar Patrika*, June 23, 2006.
18. The survey was conducted in late July, 2004. The boys interviewed were from the southern part of the city of Kolkata. Some details of these interviews have been given in *Bharate Shishusramer Rakampher*, an essay printed in a Bengali magazine, namely *Sharadpatra* published in Oct. 2004.

they found employment in various places mentioned earlier and slept on the pavements of Kolkata streets. One of them named Dulal confessed that he was happy working in a garage earning between Rs. 5/- and Rs. 10/- a day because he could now afford loaves of bread (Rs. 2/-) and *Aloo Dum* (Potato curry cooked with hot spices) sold in Kolkata streets at Rs. 3/- per bowl. So, Dulal, a permanent pavement dweller and transport worker was happy to buy the food of his choice after his liberation from bondage. A boy of 13, he had no memory of his parents or his native village in Bihar wherefrom he was brought to Kolkata by a crowded train long time back. He, however, faintly remembers a devastating flood which possibly rendered him homeless. We did not have a clue whether he was orphaned by the flood. But we came across another boy of the same group named Badal, aged about 11, whose parents died in a devastating famine in Kalahandi, Orissa. Yet another painful story was that of Bablu, a boy ten years old, who was possibly forsaken as an illegitimate child when he was barely one month old. Bablu was rescued from the Kolkata Esplanade by a beggar couple and reared by them for some years. At the age of 7 or 8 he was employed by a tea stall owner of Southern Avenue, Kolkata. No less shocking was the story of his mate Haran from Namkhana (South 24 Parganas, West Bengal) who narrated how his parents were separated when he was barely 5 years old. At first his father had gone missing. Soon after his mother also left home never to return again. It also transpired that Bablu's parents were not very poor. He was rendered homeless because his parents were separated. He became a street urchin at the age of five and sometime after got a job in a tea stall.

In the eighties and nineties of the last century, there were numerous shoe shine boys in one of the largest railway terminals of Tamilnadu, namely Madras central station.[19] Many of them could speak as many as three languages — Tamil, Telugu and Malayalam. In addition to that some of them spoke a few words of English, Hindi and Bengali. This polyglot group would astonish anybody visiting the station for the first time. They would easily distinguish the passengers from distant cities like Delhi (predominantly Hindi speaking) and Kolkata (by and large Bengali speaking) from those of the southern cities and follow them shouting "money cheap Sir, clean shoe — one rupee — one rupee." They would speak English, Hindi, Bengali, Tamil, Telugu or Malayalam determining the language a prospective customer spoke. Thus a few words of an unknown tongue would endear them to passengers from far off places. They earned very little — somewhere between Rs. 10 and Rs. 15 a day and all of them were undernourished children below fifteen years. Those children are grown up by now if they have survived the diseases related to malnutrition.

Malnutrition

We should not fail to note here that each year thousands of children of different age groups die of ailments caused by malnutrition. An Indian daily has recently provided some information in this respect which appalled the readers:[20]

> One of India's most prosperous states has revealed a horrifying underbelly. More than 9000 tribal children below the age of six have died of malnourishment-related causes in 15 districts of Maharashtra in about a year.
>
> Government statistics released on Monday acknowledged that the deaths in these areas, some close to the country's

---

19. These boys were interviewed for the first time in December, 1986. I saw no less than thirty such shoe-shine boys, all of whom were malnourished and ill-clad.

20. *The Times of India*, Kolkata, July 6, 2004.

ritziest metropolis, Mumbai, occurred between April 2003 and May this year. Between April and May this year alone, 1041 children have died. The toll until April was 7970.

The state's top health official said, however, all the deaths are not related to malnutrition.

"There are a variety of factors, including low birth weight, jaundice, convulsions, hypothermia and premature delivery," said state's director, health service, Dr. Subhash Salunke.

These figures have emerged out of a government survey. In April – May 2004, 80% children have died in five districts of Thane, Nasik, Amravati, Nandurbar and Gadchiroli alone.

Dr Salunke sought to downplay the shocking statistics by observing that the number who have died form less than 2% of the tribal child population. He said the Government was tackling the "socio-economic component" of the problem by treating adolescent anaemia and other factors. According to UNICEF figures, about 2.3 million children under the age of five die annually in India, half of these deaths due to malnutrition. Dr. Salunke's figure of 2% would thus be several times the national average.

Amar Jesani, trustee of NGP Centre for Enquiry into Health and Allied Themes (CEHAT), said malnourished children are found to be vulnerable to diseases like jaundice.

The Government does not accept malnutrition to be the cause of these deaths since it becomes a political liability. The government should treat the basic cause of these deaths, instead of blaming them on communicable diseases which can be tackled in any way, he added.

The president of the Association for Consumer Action on Safety and Health, Dr Arun Bal, blamed the Government. "There are proofs that these deaths are because of

> malnutrition. But the government is attributing the deaths to the effects of malnutrition etc. not to malnutrition per se. It is like saying a man has died of diabetes, whereas the real reason lies elsewhere. The situation is the same whichever party is in power." Dr. Bal told. . .

We have already mentioned the malnourished shoe-shine boys of Chennai (Tamilnadu). In fact Tamilnadu, like Kerala, had made some progress in its efforts to eradicate malnourishment of children:[21]

> Tamilnadu, however is an exception. The late CM, (M.G. Ramachandran) M.G.R., who went to school hungry, had resolved to eradicate hunger among children. . .
>
> . . . In Tamilnadu, it is now possible to think of feeding programmes for children as an entitlement, in the sense of a right, something accepted by society and the political leadership and which is unlucky to be questioned by reasons of resource constraints. Budgetary pressures have not led to the cutbacks in the feeding programme.

It seems worthwhile to discuss the condition in other states of India and some neighbouring countries as well, since supply of child labour to the Indian market and to the markets of West Asia through India depends also on them. In this respect India's position *vis a vis* some other underdeveloped countries invites our attention:[22]

> Today is world Food Day and 63% of all children in the country suffer from chronic malnutrition. And this too when our granaries are overflowing. The figures for chronic child malnutrition in impoverished Bangladesh is 45%, for strife-torn Rawanda 43%, for neighbouring Bhutan 40%, and for civil war-ravaged Congo 45%.

---

21. *The Times of India*, Kolkata, October 16, 2004.
22. Ibid.

The figures for underweight under-fives in India, Bangladesh, Pakistan and Nepal are 47%, 48%, 38% and 47% respectively. The average for Sub-Saharan Africa is 30%, 76% of children in Maharashtra suffer from *stunted* growth and anaemia. In Bihar 54% children are malnourished, Orissa 54% and M.P. 55%. The average for Sub-Saharan Africa is a notch less at 51%. W2hile chronic malnourishment has declined from 61.5% in 1975-79 to 47% in 2000-01, largely due to progress made by Kerala and Tamilnadu, today half the children in Kerala are mildly malnourished, a rise of 35% from 1975. Across the country mild malnourishment is rising though chronic malnutrition has shown a slight decline.

Malnutrition in Indian Children[23]

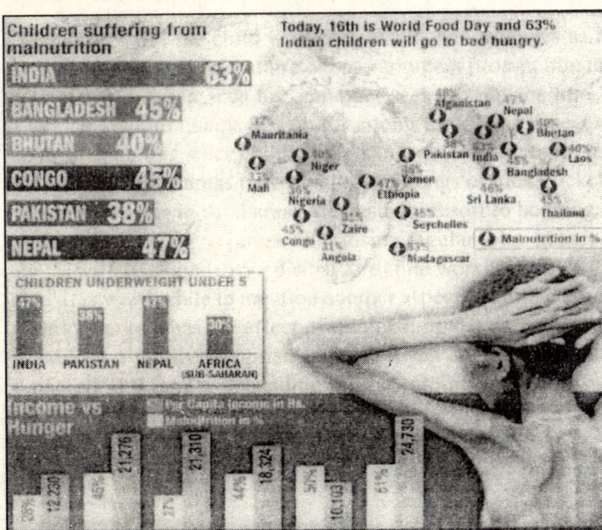

India	63%	Congo	38%
Bangladesh	45%	Zaire	31%
Bhutan	40%	Mali	33%

23. Source : *The Times of India*, Kolkata, October 16, 2004.

Pakistan	38%	Nigeria	36%
Nepal	47%	Niger	40%
Sri Lanka	46%	Angola	31%
Afghanistan	48%	Ethiopia	47%
Thailand	45%	Yemen	46%
Laos	40%		

Interestingly, malnourishment of children is not attributable to low per capita income alone. We know there are states in India where per capita income didn't greatly affect nourishment of children:[24]

> Malnourishment in children has little to do with per capita income. Manipur has a per capita income of Rs. 12230 and 28% malnutrition. Gujarat with a per capita income of Rs. 21276 has a figure of 45%. Similarly, Orissa's figure is 50% at a per capita income of Rs. 10103 while Maharashtra which has a per capita income of Rs. 24736 has malnutrition levels of 51%. Kerala's per capita income is Rs. 21310 and that of Karnataka Rs. 18324 while their malnutrition levels are 27% and 44% respectively.

This phenomenon is sometimes explained in terms of glaring income disparities in the prosperous states. But there are other reasons behind greater malnourishment levels in those states. Rapid urbanisation[25] has changed the food habits of many in the slums of Maharashtra and Gujarat. Junk food is becoming

---

24. Ibid.
25. Maharashtra, Gujarat, Karnataka, Kerala and West Bengal are among the most urbanised states in India. Kalyan in Maharashtra with a decennial growth of 645.4% is the fastest growing town in India according to census of India 1991. Asansol (108.7%) in West Bengal, Thane (105.9%) and Aurangabad (87.7%) in Maharashtra occupy respectively the second, third and fourth places — See *The Statesman*, Kolkata, October 22, 1988.

increasingly popular in urban areas including the slums. While the undernourished boy in Assam or Manipur will happily eat a banana offered by his parents, a child from a Mumbai slum will insist on some fast food prepared in a roadside eatery which obviously has very low nutrition value. So, rapid urbanization and a transformed consumption pattern have something to do with the problem of child malnutrition in the more prosperous states. It would not be out of place here to mention that so far we have spotted only a few child workers from the north-eastern states with low per capita incomes, working in other regions. Some Assamese boys and girls are found working in other north eastern states like Mizoram, Manipur and Nagaland.[26] But they do not usually migrate to other regions in search of work. Contrarily, we have identified children from West Bengal and Tamilnadu working in the Andaman and Nicobar islands, far away from the mainland.

Economy of Child Labour

Next we come to another important aspect of child labour in India. More often than not a child worker changes his profession as he grows up, without ever developing skill at a particular work. So in the labour market he is always at the receiving end. This phenomenon is essentially linked to the economy of child labour. It is unbelievably cheap as we have seen heretofore. But the child worker demands better wages as he grows up. His consumption of food and clothes and the allure of entertainment prompt him to bargain over his wages. Unwilling to satisfy his demands his employer seeks to replace him by another child. Therefore a child worker seldom retains his job for a long time. This aspect of child labour is considered most appalling since the child workers thrown out of

26. We have met many such boys from Assam working in other north-eastern states like Mizoram, Manipur and Nagaland.

employment often indulge in criminal activities. In the urban areas they usually join gangs of pick-pockets, muggers, drug traffickers, shop lifters etc. While in rural areas they usually resort to begging for survival. One also comes across children working as pimps after losing regular jobs. In fact most juveniles in conflict with the law, as we have found to our dismay, are child workers thrown out of employment or school drop-outs.[27] It is worthwhile to mention another aspect of child labour. Employment of a huge number of child workers has the effect of diminishing the demand for adult workers in the job market. Therefore, a family comprising unemployed adults and employed children is usually poorer compared to a family depending on the earnings of gainfully employed adult workers.

Now we take up for discussion some curious forms of child labour, possibly unknown in other parts of the world.

The Retrievers

In Kolkata we come across child bus ticket retrievers in major railway or bus terminals. They collect tickets thrown away by the passengers after the journey is over. These tickets are sold to numerous salesmen and other workers of both private and government organizations who are required to travel frequently. Such people often walk through the lanes and bye lanes of the city or hitchhike to their destinations thereby saving the bus or train fare. But they are in need of used tickets for claiming the fare from their employers. So the ticket retriever boy comes in handy usually claiming a commission

---

27. About children in conflict with the law, two reports published in *The Times of India* (Kolkata) of October 12, 2004 and October 19, 2004 respectively, provide interesting information. On October 19, was published a report on abduction of a trader in Kolkata by school drop-outs.

Child workers rolling *bidi*.

Child workers rolling *bidi*.

Deluged by a flood.

Destitute children of a flood ravaged village. (Courtesy: B. Roy)

Agricultural Labourer

The Domestic help. (Courtesy: Somen Bera)

as high as 10% of the value of the ticket. For railway tickets, particularly those for long distance the rate is even higher.

Another type of child workers are engaged in sieving water and solid waste in the gutters located near large shops of gold and silver ornament manufacturers and jewellers. Such workers can be spotted in the crowded streets of Kolkata, Mumbai, Surat, Delhi, Ahmedabad, Pune, Lucknow and many other cities where there are jewellery and ornament manufacturers. In fact, a town with a sizeable *Sonapatty* almost invariably attracts them. But in this trade also the child workers labour for a pittance. At times the children succeed in retrieving small pearls, gold and silver rings, gold dust etc. Group leaders collect the retrieved articles from the child workers and arrange for their sale in the market. Formerly a community called *Nehariwalla* monopolized this trade who would often engage their children in sifting mud and solid waste from the gutters under the supervision of the elders of the community. The *Nehariwalla* is possibly on the verge of extinction.[28]

There are children who retrieve coins thrown into the holy rivers like the Ganga or other water bodies in the immediate vicinity of the holy shrines. Religious festivals attract large number of pilgrims and devotees to the shrines and the children then have a good haul. This is undoubtedly one of the hazardous works since some of the children are drowned by the high tide in the Ganga every year. Other water bodies too are not safe either.

Some children earn their livelihood by retrieving structures and backslabs of clay idols of deities after their immersion in the water bodies. Such immersion takes place once the *puja* of

---

28. Information about the *Nehariwallas* were collected from different districts of Bihar, U.P. and West Bengal.

the deity is over. Dresses and ornaments of the idols are also retrieved. Structures of smaller images can fetch between Rs. 15 and 35 while a big image like that of Durga can be worth Rs. 200. In the festive season of September/October a boy retriever can earn nearly Rs. 200.[29] The trade is usually a preserve of the children of slums and villages on the shores of rivers.[30]

A group of retrievers can be seen in the cremation grounds also. They retrieve cinders from the funeral pyres. The cinders so collected are finely crushed and used as basic raw material for manufacturing incense sticks. In the city of Patna, nearly one hundred children work in a crematorium named Bansghat.[31] They do odd jobs around day in and day out.

One of the extremely hazardous professions was that of a gully pit boy of the Kolkata Metropolitan Corporation. He would remove the mud from the underground gutters through small manholes, very often risking his life inhaling noxious fumes. This particular form of labour has long been prohibited. But a Kolkata street named after a certain Nafar Chandra Kundu who scarificed his life trying to rescue a gully pit boy from a sewer, sometime in the early twentieth century, would remind us of the hazardous profession and its poor victims.[32]

In the *sabjimandi*s of Delhi, Kolkata, Mumbai and other big cities we come across some child workers who retrieve vegetables from the bins and the gutters. The things so

---

29. *Anandabazar Patrika*, October 25, 2004.
30. It is extremely hazardous on October 25, Alpha Bangla, a TV Channel, reported the death of a child retriever at Rishra, WB.
31. *The Hindustan Times*, July 2, 2006.
32. A sweeper boy aged 10, was drowned in a municipal cistern in the Padmapukur (Kerani Bagan) in 1904 — See for details *The Statesman*, November 08, 1904.

retrieved are sold in the market at a cheaper rate by a different group of vendors who are not allowed to sell them inside the market proper. They instead occupy the sidewalks in the close vicinity of the markets. The children engaged in this trade are niggardly paid and can barely manage two meals a day.

Other Forms of Child Labour

In the railway compartments, particularly of the mail and express trains, a class of child workers are seen with broom in hand. They are self-appointed sweepers earning an occasional tip from the willing passenger.[33] Interviewing a few such boys we have gathered that they earn very little a day. Possibly this is not an organized trade as we don't have any information about group leaders collecting the money from the sweeper children. Sometime back, a ten year old self appointed boy sweeper was electrocuted at Adra railway station (Purulia, W.B.) while trying to retrieve his bag of coins thrown on the roof of a railway compartment by his friend. This was just a bit of fun but the poor boy, ignorant of the consequences, climbed the roof and was electrocuted. The boy and his friends lived at the railway platform of Adra.[34]

Another class of child workers, namely the *Punkha* pullers have almost gone into oblivion. Indeed *punkha*[35] pulling was not a preserve of the child workers alone since adults were also employed as *punkha*-pullers. Before the advent of

33. *The Times of India*, in a report published on April 3, 2005 provided some information about the sweeper boys.

34. See for details — *The Anandabazar Patrika*, December 18, 2004.

35. *Hobson-Jobson*, the glossary of colonial Anglo-Indian words and phrases, published in 1886, defines *Punkha* as a large fixed and swinging fan, formed of cloth stretched in a rectangular frame and suspended from the ceiling, which is used to agitate the air in hot weather.

electricity *punkha*s were indispensable in wealthy homes and office buildings. They were swung by hand or leg. When the worker was tired he would pull the *punkha* by a leg, lying on his back.

Manufacturing of explosive fireworks is one of the most hazardous professions employing child workers in India.[36] Sivakasi in Tamilnadu is one of the most important centres of this trade. None can give an exact estimate of the number of children engaged in this profession. There are smaller centres distributed all over India employing numerous children. Kalyani, an industrial town near Kolkata has four manufacturing units mostly dependent on child labour. In some Indian states restrictions have been imposed on sale of explosive fireworks causing sound pollution. These have brought about a recession in this industry in recent times.

In West Bengal, Bihar, U.P., Jharkhand, Orissa and Assam a very large number of children are employed in the brick fields. They are recruited through agents called *arkathi*s or *dalal*s who receive the wages on behalf of the group of workers consisting of adult males, females and children. The agents receive a hefty commission, sometimes as high as 25% of the wage of a worker. The payments are usually made in three or four instalments. The boy worker receives Rs. 40/- a day on an average which is less than a dollar. They are employed for seven or eight months a year because brick is manufactured only in the dry season and during the rainy season the workers go back to their native villages in far-off places.[37]

---

36. An explosion in a Srikakulam (Andhra Pradesh) fire works factory in November 2004, claimed more than ten lives — See for details *Deccan Chronicle,* Hyderabad, November 5, 2004.

37. For information about brick field workers I am indebted to Goutam Bhattacharyya of Krishnagar (Nadia dist., West Bengal).

Many children in India also work in the construction projects. The skilled boy mason who assist the adults in carrying or laying brick earn between Rs. 50 and 60 in urban areas. Since there is adequate supply of labour, the workers seldom get employment for the whole year. The boy worker in the construction project nevertheless is better off in comparison with the children employed in other fields. A mine worker for example, is more distressed and prone to diseases. A child worker of a Haryana mine has recently suffered from silicosis and died at his home at Kushmandi, West Bengal.[38]

There are numerous child rickshaw pullers in the cities of India while far greater is the number of child peddlers whom we can find in every Indian city. The average daily income of a child rickshaw-puller in Kolkata is nearly Rs. 50/- while that of a peddler is Rs. 30/- only. The former has to pay a rent to the owner of the rickshaw while the latter is totally under the control of the *mahajan*[39] since he has no capital to invest.

Jugglery, rope walking, acrobatics etc. are among the professions employing large number of children in India. Magic as a profession in India dates from way back, the ancient period to be precise. Acrobatics is hazardous at times for it may lead to accidents and fatal injury. A child acrobat is employed by a circus or a professional group of entertainers who travel far and wide in search of business. Circus is more popular in the rural areas but child acrobats and jugglers can still be seen in the vast sea beaches of Mumbai and Chennai, the Esplanade of Kolkata and parks and gardens of many other Indian cities. These children are also ill-paid but not as ill-fed and ill-clad like the rag pickers or shoe-shine boys.

---

38. See for details — *The Anandabazar Patrika,* December 25, 2004.
39. The term has various connotations e.g. Moneylender, banker, merchant etc. Here it is taken to mean moneylender.

In some big cities of India one would come across the florist child waiting for the traffic signal at major intersections. When the cars stop the florist children rush to them with flowers, garlands and bouquets in their hands. On festive or auspicious days they make handsome profit. Interestingly, this profession has now become popular in rural India also. A person travelling from Kolkata to Siliguri in Northern Bengal once too often come across the florists at a number of places like Bethuadahari and Berhampur. We have not been able to estimate their daily earnings. But it goes up during winter when they take part in cultivation of flowers.

In the fish markets of Kolkata a large number of children are employed in scraping the scales from the fish bought by the customers. On an average they earn Rs. 15 a day which is equivalent to nearly one third of a dollar, working for five to six hours a day. Most of them, as we are told, are school drop-outs and some of them are as young as seven or eight.

Child Prostitution

Abominable forms of child labour in India include child prostitution which has assumed alarming proportions in recent times. Robert I. Freidman observes that it takes upto 15 years for girls held in prostitution, via debt bondage to purchase their freedom.[40] Delhi, Mumbai, Kolkata, Chennai, Bangalore, Hyderabad, Agra and Lucknow are most reputed for harbouring flesh trade. In some Indian cities like Lucknow urchins work as pimps in red light areas. Apart from the poorer rural areas of India some neighbouring countries like Nepal, Bangladesh and Bhutan contribute to this trade to a

40. See for details — Robert I, Freidman, "India's Shame : Sexual Slavery and Political Corruption are Leading to an AIDS Catastrophe," *The Nation*, April 8, 1996.

great extent.[41] Child prostitution in India had a long history and its causes are deep-rooted. One of the earliest references to this trade can be found in the account of Ibn Batuta, an Arab traveller visiting Bengal, in the fourteenth century. Batuta bought a beautiful slave girl during his sojourn in Bengal.

Child prostitution in India is usually attributed to extreme poverty:[42]

> Extreme poverty is the reason and prostitution the result. Unable to combat the crisis, a large number of minor girls (below 18 years of age), mainly from the backward classes and minority community, join the flesh trade in Birbhum every year.
>
> A survey done for over the past four years, starting from 2000, in Bolpur, Suri, Sainthia, Nalhati and Paikar in the district, by a Santiniketan based NGO, Elmhirst Institute of Community Studies, revealed the fact. The project was funded by the West Bengal State AIDS Prevention and Control Society.
>
> Within its project area, the NGO located 278 minor girls, to have entered the flesh trade. Of these, a majority belongs to the backward classes and minority groups (Scheduled caste, 3.7 per cent, scheduled tribe, 6 per cent, minority community, 42 per cent).
>
> The NGO, however, did not include the flying sex workers. The report reads: "The flying sex workers are supplementing their income by entering into the profession. They are hidden and it is very difficult to locate them as they do not come forward." Based on the number of minor girls who have joined the trade in the project area, the report estimated that about 1600 minor girls have already entered the profession

41. *The Times of India*, Kolkata, September 18, 2004.
42. *The Statesman*, Kolkata, Septemebr 13, 2004.

in the entire district. The report also mentioned that the actual number may cross a few thousands if a proper survey is done throughout the district.

The survey conducted by the Elmhirst Institute of Community Studies was confined to the district of Birbhum alone. But in other districts of West Bengal also minor-girl trafficking is on the rise. In a recent report published in a Kolkata daily some such areas have been mentiond:[43]

> Within West Bengal too, areas from where large number of women are sent off to other places are mainly, Murshidabad, Midnapore (east and west), South and North 24 Parganas, Birbhum, Burdwan, Malda, Nadia and South and North Dinajpur.

Investigation about international rackets engaged in minor girl trafficking has revealed harrowing stories:[44]

> Thirteen-year old Sabina (name changed) left her village at Gazipur, Bangladesh to study in Kolkata only because her neighbour and uncle Iftab Hussain wanted her to do it. Little did she know that her school would actually be a brothel. She is one of the hundreds residing in a Sonagachi[45] by-lane.
>
> Sabina is not alone. According to statistics collected by the non-governmental organization Socio-legal Aid Research and Training Centre (SLARTC), nearly 10,000 women are trafficked from Bangladesh[46] and a similar number from adjoining countries like Nepal and Bhutan to Kolkata and parts of West Bengal every year.

---

43. *The Times of India*, Kolkata, September 18, 2004.
44. Ibid.
45. A red light district of Kolkata.
46. *The Jugantar;* a Dhaka daily, has reported abduction of two minor girls from Sialmari village of Madhabpur sub-district — See for details *The Jugantar*, December 26, 2003.

> Nearly 15 per cent of those trafficked are below the age of 15 and 25 per cent are below 18 years. In fact overall in India, over 40,000 children are victims of commercial sexual exploitation.
>
> These corroborate the international migration statistics which states that out of the 175 million people migrating from one country to another, at least 48 per cent happen to be women who are victims of sexual exploitation. . .
>
> . . .Most traffickers use Kolkata as a transit point. "At least five to ten per cent of these girls coming from Bangladesh and one per cent from Nepal stay back in the city's red light areas". . . .
>
> . . .Most women trafficked from Bangladesh are sent to Pakistan and thereafter to West Asian countries while girls from Nepal and Bhutan are sent to Mumbai and north eastern states.

The Human Rights Commission in a recently published report has expressly mentioned that girls are trafficked to West Bengal from different states of India.[47]

The report has identified some transit points for girl trafficking in those states. Gorakhpur and Lucknow in U.P., Baleswar and Bhadrak in Orissa and Solapur in Maharashtra are among such points. Kathmandu & Nepalganj in Nepal and Dhaka, Jessore, Pabna, Coomilla and Khulna in Bangladesh are among the cities which figure in the list of centres of girls-trafficking. Mention may also be made here of the fact that the traffickers often utilize their political connections for protection against police actions.[48] All round corruption perpetuate the crime. Innocent minors are usually duped by

47. *The Anandabazar Patrika*, October 13, 2004.
48. *The Statesman*, Kolkata, October 17, 2004.

their relatives who traffic them to brothels as we have seen in the case mentioned below:[49]

> Mafuza has the dreamy eyes of any 13 year old girl. Her parents work in a brick kiln and her only brother is fighting a losing battle against blood cancer. And when a relative offered to help her find a job, her joy knew no bounds. But it all turned to be trauma when she realized, rather lately, what her cousin was up to.
>
> In two months from July this year this girl from North 24 Parganas was sold and resold seven times in the brothels of Mumbai. Mafuza has six other friends who share the same plight — all are underage girls rescued by the Madhyamgram-based NGO, Centre for Communication and Development, from brothels across the country.
>
> Most of the minors were tricked by their relatives with promise of jobs.
>
> In the case of Anwara Khatun, who is from Kalipur, her aunt and the first cousin were the traffickers who sold the girl to a tout in Mumbai who later pressured her into prostitution. This seventeen year old still has scars of her sadistic customers— blade bruises and cigarette-burnt marks all over her body.
>
> A neighbour was instrumental in Raima's (13) landing up in a Mumbai brothel. On getting the information, Raima's mother rushed to Mumbai to bring her daughter back only to be beaten up by brothel-runners.
>
> Sabita Parui, another resident of Deganga fell prey to traffickers posing as recruiters. And she ended up in a Delhi brothel before she was rescued by the NGO with police help. The NGO office-bearers, however, decry the lack of help from police in bringing the culprits to book.

49. Ibid.

A trafficker in the guise of a benefactor is indeed dangerous. A girl child in India is not necessarily safe at the hands of the so-called benevolent organizations of which there has been a mushroom growth in recent times. A notice issued by the Supreme Court of India to the government of West Bengal and an NGO was an eye-opener. It concerned a petition alleging that the NGO had been running a sex racket involving minor girls in West Bengal in collusion with the police.[50]

> The court issued the notice to the West Bengal home secretary and the NGO *Sanlaap* on a special leave petition alleging that the NGO had been collecting "only beautiful minor girls" in nexus with the police who had been, in turn accusing "poor and illiterate women" of indulging in prostitution and separating their daughters from them. These minor girls are then handed over to the NGO which holds them malafide for years together, the petition alleged. The charges were being made without any material evidence to substantiate the allegation against these women, the petition further stated. The petition cited the instance of one Mrs Simla Singh whose minor daughter Juhi was separated from her after police arrested Mrs Singh in an alleged false criminal case and handed Juhi over to *Sanlaap*. The petition sought restoration of the daughter's custody to the mother.
>
> The home was only intended to have temporary custody of only one month, the petition further stated. But Juhi was kept at the home for over a year in an "uncared condition" and her education discontinued, the SLP said. Mrs Singh's SLP was against a high court order denying her any relief. Advocate for the petitioner Mr Bijay Adhikari said he would file more petitions in the Supreme Court soon drawing its attention to several other such instances in Bengal.

---

50. *The Statesman*, Kolkata, October 28, 2004.

Child prostitution is rampant in some other states as well. In another sensational incident an interstate girl-trafficking racket was busted and eight minor girls were rescued from brothels of Pune and Mumbai. Of them seven were from South 24 Parganas in West Bengal and one was from Murshidabad of the same state.[51] International girl trafficking rackets also deserve mention. In fact luring Indian girls to West Asia after promising them jobs as domestic helps is becoming increasingly common.

> Two such gibrls, one from Andhra Pradesh and another from Kerala who have been rescued are waiting for travel documents to be sent back home.[52]
>
> "Most of the agents are form Kerala and most of the girls are from Andhra Pradesh, Karnataka and Kerala," an Indian consulate official said. Many are brought here on fake promises of jobs and then forced into the sex racket. The consulate is currently preparing for the protection of emigrants so as to prevent the agents in sex rackets from luring girls to the Gulf.
>
> Three months ago a minor girl was rescued in pitiable conditions. . .the girls hardly get any money as the lion's share of income is pocketed by these agents.

Whether in India or in West Asia the girls live in abject poverty and squalor, almost completely shut off from the world outside the brothel. Their proneness to diseases is well-known. When they grow older or fall sick they initiate their minor daughters into the profession.

The Domestic Helps

For a minor girl in India, forced to eke out an existence on her

---

51. *The Times of India*, September 28, 2004.
52. *The Statesman*, Kolkata, September 13, 2004.

own, the job of a housemaid is often considered a safer option. But we have several instances of their being brutally tortured by the employers. In October 2004, a twelve year old girl was rescued from a house in Kestopur near Kolkata by her neighbours. She was mercilessly beaten up several times on one pretext or the other.[53]

No better is the condition of a minor boy working as a domestic help. There are instances galore. In June 2004, a young boy named Prasanta Nayak was rescued by Orissa police from the house of his employer, a scion of the erstwhile ruling family of Kheria in the district of Nuapara. The eight-year-old boy bore several injuries inflicted on him by his employer's wife. As it caused a great sensation, the chief minister of Orissa had ordered an enquiry into the incident.[54]

Scholars and social workers have so far attributed the steady supply of child labour to poverty alone. But in depth enquiries have revealed a few more factors which deserve our attention.

i. Abduction of Children by racketeers especially from city slums or backward regions.

ii. Premature death of their parents or supportive kin due to epidemic or natural disaster.

iii. Displacement of children caused by separation of parents.

iv. Abandonment of illegitimate children.

v. Emotional problems caused by inadequate care, maladjustment with environment and physical and mental abuse suffered by them.

---

53. *The Anandabazar Patrika* October 4, 2004.

54. *The Anandabazar Patrika*, June 16, 2004.

In fact we have not so far seriously addressed ourselves to these problems since poverty, considered as the singlemost important factor behind the wretched condition of millions of children in India has absorbed much of our attention. But unless these factors are taken care of along with poverty, abolition of child labour in India will remain a far cry.

Already appallingly high, the number of child workers in India is increasing by leaps and bounds. But people who employ them seldom give correct information as to their number, age and status during census operations. So collecting correct information about child labour has hitherto remained a ticklish task for the census workers in India.[55] In a revealing statement made in 2000 the law minister of India mentioned that there were about twenty million child workers in India.[56] Despite being a conservative estimate it is immensely disquieting to us as we are yet to formulate a definite policy on child labour and child rights.

---

55. In a report published in November, 2004, it has been elaborately discussed. The focus was on collection of data on age — See for details. *The Times of India*, Kolkata, November 1, 2004.

56. *The Indian Express*, February 2, 2004.

3

Child Abuse in India and the SAARC Countries

Feel the dignity of a child,
Do not feel superior to him, for you are not.

— Robert Henri

In India the and the SAARC Countrie problem of child abuse has assumed massive proportions in recent times. Considered an impediment to development it is an issue warmly debated. What constitutes a child abuse is also a moot question. Broadly speaking, it's the offence causing physical or emotional injury on a child. It includes verbal abuse, failure to furnish proper shelter, nourishment, medical treatment or emotional support; sexual molestation and any sort of violence done to a child.[1]

In Europe it was in the eighteenth century, the age of enlightenment, that people began to adopt ideas of humanism and along with it came the concept of child care in a much broader sense. Ironically, children suffered most in the next century when industrial mass production required employment of children on a large scale in the factories.[2] Through passage of time, child abuse came in for widespread condemnation in

1. *Britannica Ready Reference Encyclopedia*, vol. II, p. 231 New Delhi, 2004.
2. John Whitney Hall (Ed.), *History of the World : The Renaissance to the World War I*, pp. 77 ff, Greenwich, 1988.

Europe and the USA But in India and other third world countries it continued unabated.

The baneful effect of child abuse can hardly be exaggerated. The trauma suffered in childhood may find expression in bizarre behavior at different stages of life. It has also been found in many cases that the abuser himself has experienced the trauma of abuse.[3] Unpleasant experience buried deep in the subconscious may lead to perverse manifestations in later life.

But an average Indian doesn't regard child abuse as inhuman or immoral. There are numerous instances.

When about a few years back a young Indian couple was apprehended by the police in a large departmental stores of a central European state for brutally assaulting their child who wanted to buy a precious toy, they had virtually no idea that child abuse was banned in that state.[4] Although they were repentant for their unsavoury conduct, the repercussions were unpleasant. Through prolonged entreaties they were able to get rid of the charge of child abuse. Unfortunately many people in India are on the same footing as the above mentioned couple with regard to child rights. Let's look at a recent case reported from Orissa:[5]

> Dipika Depanjali (17), the missing schoolgirl traced in Gujarat. . .alleged that, due to regular physical and mental torture by her father, she had fled home in frustration.
>
> After her arrival in Bhubaneswar with a police team, Dipika also put an end to the abduction claim made by her father,

---

3. *Britannica Ready Reference Encyclopedia,* Loc. cit.
4. Interview with S. Alam, May 1999.
5. *The Hindustan Times,* Kolkata, February 14, 2005.

J.N. Biswal. Since January 31, Dipika had gone missing and Biswal lodged a complaint of kidnapping.

He also told the police that two Oriya youths kept Dipika in Valsad district of Gujarat and they demanded ransom from him over the telephone.

During the rescue operation, the two youths — Ashok Sahu and Kishan Pradhan — were detained by the police and brought to Bhubaneswar along with the girl.

The youths hail from the Dhamnagar area of Bhadrak district and were working as labourers in a cotton mill of Surat.

Dipika told reporters, "On my own, I'd left home to avoid the regular physical and mental torture by my father. It was also difficult for me to witness the regular torture of my mother. Even now I am not willing to return home.

About the two detained youths she said, "They helped me a lot while I was travelling in a distressed condition on the Mumbai-bound Konark express. They saved me from a group of notorious youths and gave me shelter in their Krishna colony residence. The duo treated me as their younger sister and it's only because of them that I am back here safely.

One of the detained youths, Ashok Sahu, ruled out the allegation that they demanded ransom from Dipika's father, but said, "we had only asked him for the expenses incurred by us in bringing the girl to Gujarat and keeping her in our house."

He added, "We tried to take the girl back to her parents, but she threatened to commit suicide if we did that."

Going by the girl's version, the police have stopped investigating the kidnapping angle.

Biswal had in fact concocted an elaborate story of abduction of his daughter to cover up his misdeed. No wonder social stigma attached to such incidents prompted him to do so.

Our next case is that of a child committing suicide by hanging himself from a beam of his house. This boy, aged about 12, got a scolding from his mother for returning late for his lunch. The school drop-out, deeply shocked as he was deprived of his lunch, committed suicide within an hour of his return. The young boy had to do all the domestic chores including cooking the lunch for the whole family.[6] None the less he was not allowed to take a few hours off to play or chat with his friends which was quite becoming of a child of his age. This was a case of extreme negligence and tyranny on the part of the parents of the hapless boy against which he had no protection.

Adopted children often suffer brutal abuse at the hands of their so-called legal parents. Fake adoption make the life of a child a misery. The case of 8 year old Payel from Bandel, West Bengal, was an eye opener. At the age of five, she was adopted by a couple from a rescue home. Soon after, she was severely beaten up by them. The little girl was forced to do all household chores throughout the day. As she was regularly tortured, her neighbours lodged a complaint with the police the very first year she went to her adopted home. Promise of good behaviour in future resulted in withdrawal of the charges. But it erupted again after three years when her neighbours found that the child was abused as before and locked up for most part of the day.[7]

---

6. *The Anandabazar Patrika,* February 21, 2005.

7. *The Anandabazar Patrika,* December 17, 2004.

This case is illustrative of the fact that a girl child is often adopted to substitute for a domestic help. In big cities like Kolkata, Mumbai or Delhi domestic helps demand better wages which many people find unaffordable. For them fake adoption of an orphaned girl come in handy.

In most parts of India child abuse is so rampant in schools that it demands immediate attention of the government. Sometimes flimsy excuse is offered when a case of child abuse catches attention of the people.

> It was meant to be punishment for fiddling with the principal's car. But in the end it backfired with students being hospitalized and some parents and the principal spending the night behind bars.
>
> Several students fell ill at Barisa Vivekananda Girl's School on Diamond Harbour Road in Thakurpukur after principal Ila Samaddar made them stand in the sun for hours after the morning prayers. She was punishing them for fiddling with her car in school. She wasn't sure who did it. So she punished all the Class VIII and Class IX students (nearly 200). A dozen odd students fell ill, four of them down with dehydration.
>
> When parents got to know what was going on, they went on the rampage in the school, breaking windows and heckling the principal. They even attacked cops. Police arrested 14 parents and later Samaddar and School Secretary Asim Ghosh.[8]

Samaddar's plea was that, she as a physically challenged person, couldn't move without the car and for the past few days someone was putting food waste inside her car. She asked the students about it and no one owned up.

8. *The Times of India*, Kolkata, February 12, 2005.

Consequently, she punished the girls the way we have mentioned heretofore.

Sometimes unique methods are applied for punishing the students :[9]

> A student at a primary school in Maharashtra's Beed district was kept dangling in a well by his teacher because he failed to sing film songs. Rural development minister Vijay Singh Mohite Patil said the incident took place on February 4. The teacher, who threatened four other students that he would throw them into the well, has been apprehended.

Singing of film songs was not on the curriculum of the school. It was the whim of a particular teacher that led to trouble. There was no one around to prevent the teacher from inflicting such brutal punishment on the students. There are however, instances of punishments cruller in nature :[10]

> Spare the hair, spoil the child! Despite periodic court strictures against the practice, corporal punishment in schools is alive and kicking.
>
> Five-year-old Varnika Gupta of nursery section A, at Our Lady Queen of the Mission School in Salt Lake, had a tuft of hair uprooted by class teacher. . . .because she had forgotten to bring a plastic carry bag to school. The teacher had told Varnika and her classmates that they must bring a bag each to carry back home some artwork assignments.
>
> It was Varnika's bad luck that she had forgotten this all-important bag. . . (The Teacher) who saw it as a sure sign of intransigence, flew into a rage and decided to teach the kid a lesson she would remember forever. To make it doubly

---

9. *The Times of India,* Kolkata, April 13, 2005.
10. *The Hindustan Times,* Kolkata, March 17, 2005.

> certain she also made her keep standing in the classroom through the entire period.

As she returned from school the little girl told her mother about the incident. Her parents thereafter visited the school and demanded an explanation from the school authorities who refused to "entertain enquiries." Varnika's parents lodged a complaint with the police. Although the allegations were denied, the teacher was arrested by the police and soon enlarged on bail. It would also seem that the police had soft-pedalled the issue :[11]

> The teacher could have been booked under section 326 of the IPC, which is a non-bailable offence, but was charged under the less severe section 325 which is bailable. Both sections deal with corporal punishment, with 326 reserved for grievous injury. The police apparently thought pulling out a child's hair was not grievous enough.
>
> . . . (The teacher) was also charged under sections 341 (wrongful restraint), 323 and 506 (criminal intimidation), but faced no hurdles in securing a release.

Varnika was not required to undergo prolonged institutional treatment for her injury. But in some other cases the injuries inflicted on the students were so serious that they had to be rushed to hospital:

> A student was admitted to Howrah General Hospital in a serious condition today after he was allegedly beaten up by his school teacher for failing to come to class on time.
>
> Binoy Roy (16), Class IX student, Kulakamini High School of Bhatnagar, Liluah, was admitted to the hospital with breathing problems.

---

11. *The Hindustan Times,* Kolkata, March 18, 2005.

> His teacher allegedly beat him up yesterday for being late for class. Binoy's parents have not lodged a complaint with police. The teenager went to school around 11 A.M. yesterday. During a break between classes, he went to the school office to find out about the dates for filling up the Madhyamik Examination (School Final Exams) registration forms.
>
> On returning to class, he found that the subject teacher had already begun taking lessons. When she saw Binay, the teacher allegedly started beating him up, for not being present in the class. Hearing his cries teachers in adjoining classrooms rushed to his help.
>
> The teenager's father alleged that the school authorities had taken his son to hospital after it occurred to them that the incident might snowball. "He was given first-aid before they dropped him home late in the evening. But his condition started deteriorating from last night and (his father) had to admit him to the Howrah Hospital.[12]

In some cases, it would seem, the teachers brutally punish the students to cover up their inability to teach properly. English, Geography and Sanskrit are apparently among the subjects which often expose their weaknesses. There are instances aplenty to justify our conjecture. A Class VII student of a high school in West Bengal was hit on the head with a duster by a Sanskrit teacher of the School. Severely injured and bleeding profusely he was taken to a doctor who advised a CT Scan.[13]

In another incident a class VII student fell ill after she was cruelly punished by the English Teacher of her school. As she gave the wrong answer to a question she was ordered to do

---

12. *The Statesman*, Kolkata, August 23, 2004.
13. *The Times of India*, Kolkata, July 29, 2004.

100 sit-ups.[14] The traumatised 12-year-old returned home with high fever.

Our next case is that of a geography teacher of a south Kolkata school and one of her hapless students. The girl committed suicide and left behind a note blaming the geography teacher for her death. She wrote to her parents:[15]

> Please forgive me. It was my decision to get admitted to Kamala Girls' School. But I never dreamt I would face such a situation and be forced to take such an extreme step. I wanted to study geography. But I had no inkling that this urge would drive me towards death. The geography teacher is responsible for my death. . . I never failed. But nothing can be more unfortunate than failing because of someone's enmity.

The suicide note speaks of suffering borne by the girl. Enmity between a student and a teacher is never conducive to proper education. Worse still is the fact that in most of the schools there is no system to monitor teacher-student relationship. The transition from age-old and inhuman system of education to a modern and learner-friendly system had been inordinately sluggish in India. In many schools, students live in constant fear of violence from their teachers. Even missionary schools, enjoying wide reputation, are not essentially different. When a 14-year-old student of St. Joseph's Convent, Chandannagore, a former French colony, committed suicide in class room by hanging herself from a ceiling fan with a *chunni* (scarf), a stir was created in the area. It was alleged that she was subjected to torture by her class teacher on a regular course. When she was promoted to a higher class and a fresh academic session started in April 2005, the girl was under the impression that

14. *The Times of India*, Kolkata, July 24, 2004.
15. *The Times of India*, Kolkata, September 17, 2004.

her class teacher would be changed. But to her consternation she had learnt that for the fresh session also she would have the same class teacher. Gripped by depression she committed suicide almost instantaneously.[16]

It is worthwhile to mention that in most of these cases the school authorities seek to downplay the incidents instead of booking the offending teachers.[17]

In the St. Joseph's Convent case, it was alleged that the deceased girl annoyed the teacher by refusing to receive private tuition from her while most of her friends did so. The reason behind her not taking private tuition was that she always scored high marks in the examinations.[18] Her intransigent attitude had affected the tuition racket run by the teachers of the school. If the example of a good student like her was followed by other students, the tuition racket would suffer considerable losses. Therefore, it would seem, the torture on her was premeditated.

Yet another case of abuse by a geography teacher reported from Basirhat, North 24 Parganas (West Bengal) led to the arrest of the offending teacher as a complaint was lodged with the local police. The victim, a 12 year old girl, was hospitalized in an unconscious state.[19]

School authorities sometimes resort to unheard of means to punish students. A case reported from Aizawl (Mizoram) was sensational:[20]

---

16. *The Telegraph*, Kolkata, April 7, 2005.
17. Ibid; *The Times of India*, Kolkata, September 17, 2004; *The Statesman*, Kolkata, April 7, 2005.
18. *The Telegraph*, Kolkata, April,7, 2005.
19. *The Times of India*, Kolkata, March 24, 2005; *The Anandabazar Patrika*, March 24, 2005.
20. *The Times of India*, Kolkata, April 15, 2005.

Had their parents enough money to pay their school fees, Lalawmpuia (7) and Lalihimpuia could have enjoyed last Christmas with friends at home. But that was not to be as the script took a tragic turn.

The two pre-teen boys instead spent not only the Christmas week but more than four gruelling months confined within the boundaries of their school at the whim of their principal. Their offence — the boys' parents could not cough up the fees for their school term on time. The principal charted his own course of draconian justice; ordering the boys' confinement till their parents would pay up.

For friends and classmates of Lalawmpuia and Lalihimpuia — both students of Goodwill Academy at Aizwal's Tlangnuam — November 5 heralded the last day of their term before school closed for Christmas and the winter vacation. With examinations having been taken care of, the little boys hopped and jumped out of their classrooms to the welcome chime of the end-of-the-day bell. There was a sea of smiling faces on the school compound as the children waved their last good-byes for the term.

But for Lalawmpuia and Lalihimpuia, their ordeal had just begun. As they watched with moist eyes their mates leave the hostel dorms one by one, their principal, Shushilo Yandkhom, made it clear to them that they will not be allowed to do so till their parents had cleared the dues to the last farthing, the amount somewhere in the region of Rs. 47,000.

Since their parents, Saithanga and Lalnunmawii, could not muster the substantial sum at such short notice, the lugubrious confines of an empty hostel dorm witnessed what emerged as perhaps the darkest Christmas hour that the boys would ever have to endure. The impecunious

> condition of their father, Saithanga, had taken its toll : "I couldn't make both ends meet. I was bankrupt, I could do nothing," he wailed.
>
> As the hours ticked inexorably and with no one to turn to, Saithanga took the matter to the Mizo Zirlai Pawl.[21] The Mizo Zirlai Pawl and the council of their village intervened instantly. Emissaries were sent to Goodwill Academy and the principal urged to abandon his harsh stand.
>
> Yandkhom was adamant : "Repeated requests were made to the parents about the outstanding. Excuse after excuse was all I got." He refused to budge. And the children wept relentlessly as the shadows lengthened on Christmas evening.

An important aspect of the cases of abuse of children in schools deserves to be discussed at some length. Parents and guardians do not usually protest against abuse, not to speak of lodging complaints with the police. Interestingly, there is a rural-urban divide in this regard.[22] In the case reported from Aizwal, initially there was no complaint lodged with the police. The parents of the boys held in captivity for so many days reported the matter to the Tribal Council only after a considerable lapse of time.[23] Social status of a man almost inexorably determines his attitude toward such abuse. Even when a child is regularly tortured by a teacher the guardian seldom protests against it if he belongs to any of the underprivileged classes. Curiously enough many illiterates in India, particularly in the rural districts, hold the view that the teachers are infallible and

21. MZP is a non-political organisation devoted to social and philanthropic activities.
22. Bhattacharya, M. S, *Bharate Sisusram,* p.59, Kolkata, 2005.
23. *The Times of India*, Kolkata, April 15, 2005.

they do everything in the interest of their students. It's in fact a legacy of ancient India when *gurus* were revered as demi-gods.

When in July 2004, a little boy of a school in Lilua (W.B.) was severely tortured by his Sanskrit teacher, his parents didn't protest because the teacher had apologized for his action.[24] But there was quite a furore when almost during the same period a schoolgirl fell ill after punishment at Santragachi (Howrah dist.) West Bengal.[25] These two students were from the same district, namely Howrah in West Bengal and presumably belonged to the same social station. Therefore apart from the rural-urban, rich-poor and literate-illiterate divides, the level of individual awareness against abuse also counts to a considerable degree.

Now let us turn to abuse perpetrated against children who are not in a position to enroll in schools and the omnipresent school drop-outs forced to work hard for the sake of livelihood. Howrah railway station, one of the biggest terminals in India, is a place where hundreds of children silently move toward death :[26]

> Drugs are catching them and killing some of them young at Howrah station. One comes across hundreds of urchins, sweeping the floors of long distance trains, picking up empty water-bottles or begging for alms. Ever wondered where the changes you offer to them are spent? These are used for buying a particular brand of glue which they pour into handkerchief and sniff in order to get a kick.

---

24. *The Times of India*, Kolkata, July 29, 2004.
25. *The Times of India*, Kolkata, July 24, 2004.
26. *The Times of India*, Kolkata, April 3, 2005.

> "I have been into this for two years. My head reels and I feel good," said Sumit Das, an orphan, barely eight years old. He picks rags to buy his tubes of glue. "I need to take sniff 10 to 15 times a day. It makes me feel drowsy and I doze off after taking my dose," said 13-year-old Santosh. "It kills the hunger in my stomach" he added.
>
> There are around 300 child drug abusers registered with *Don Bosco Ashalayam*, an NGO providing counselling to these children at the station. Around one hundred of them take shelter in the station itself and the rest come from as far as Asansol, Chengail, Tikiapara and bordering places of Bihar and Jharkhand.
>
> "Most of these children are from broken homes and have no one to look after them," said director of the *Ashalayam*, Father James Mathews.
>
> Some of these children even get killed while trying to cross the railway tracks or trying to board a running train in a drugged state. Mangal and Ratan are the latest victims.
>
> These children get into drug as early as five. Girls are equally into it, making them vulnerable to sexual exploitation.
>
> There had been instances of porters and vendors in the station molesting the girls when they were in drugged state" said the counsellor. Later on some of them are even lured into prostitution. Though these child drug users do not pose a great law and order problem at the station they get into bigger crimes latter when they graduate into harder drugs.
>
> The younger ones are basically into picking rags but the older ones get into lifting and pick-pocketing. And later some of them graduate to become big criminals, said an officer of the Government railway police.

Even more appalling was a report on sexual abuse of children in another big railway terminal, namely Sealdah in Kolkata :[27]

> Rampant sexual abuse, rape and homosexuality has given rise to increasing cases of sexually transmitted diseases among the destitute children living on railway platforms.
>
> Aged between 6 and 14, these children are exposed to abuse by vendors, porters and even elder children of the group. Some are runaway kids; others have no parents or a single parent who do not take care of them.
>
> "The early exposure to sex leads to problems. Because they are sexually abused by many people on the platforms, they stop trusting adults and eventually pick up the habits of elder children in the group". . .
>
> *Cini Asha,* an NGO that works with children living on the Howrah and Sealdah station platforms, is doing a qualitative research on their knowledge, attitude, behaviour and practice. UNICEF reports show that 25 per cent of these children have STDs. . .
>
> . . .With constant exposure to sex and abuse, the traumatised children often turn to crime.

Horrific cases of sexual abuse of children have also been reported from Goa where paedophiles patronise child prostitution.[28]

Most deplorable is the fact that no significant measures have so far been adopted to save these children from such horrific abuse. It doesn't seem to be a mammoth task for the authorities to rescue these children and provide them with food, shelter and education, particularly when it is evident that any ameliorative measure meant for these children will enlist active support from some NGOs.

---

27. *The Hindustan Times*, Kolkata, March 14, 2005.
28. See *The Anandabazar Patrika*, March 24, 2006.

Miseries of the children from the underprivileged classes do not end here. There are types of abuse, unknown in other parts of the world which they meekly suffer. One of the cruelest is what we come to next.[29]

> The police have busted a gang which kidnapped toddlers and maimed them to run a begging racket. A one year old girl was rescued during the raid in Topsia.
>
> Three members of the gang including two women, were arrested from Park Circus. The fourth is absconding.
>
> Sources in the police said Mohammed Rafique (28), the leader of the gang, ran the racket with his three wives. The four abducted children from different parts of the city and brought them to their Topsia hideout. The kids were then drugged and, while unconscious, their limbs were deformed so that they attracted the sympathy of the people. Some were also given doses of toxic compounds, which either deformed them physically or made them mentally retarded. Rafique's wives then took them to different railway stations, where they were forced to beg. Sometimes, dressed in tattered clothes, one of the women posed as a kid's mother and begged instead.
>
> The police swung into action after the father of a missing child lodged a complaint. One-year-old Sayesta Parveen disappeared from near her home at Nayabasti in Khardah, on April 2. Her father, Mohammed Sohrub, filed an FIR with the local police. The fact that Mohammad Sohrub was a poor tailor made sleuths hunt for a stronger motive behind a possible abduction than just ransom money.

29. *The Hindustan Times*, Kolkata, April 14, 2005.

> Preliminary investigations revealed that a certain Md. Rafique, who often visited Sohrub's neighbour, was sometimes seen talking to Sayesta. Some locals also tipped cops that Rafique had some dubious business in Topsia. Taking one from the information gathered at Nayabasti. . .the police chalked out a plan. . . (and) Rafique and two of his wives were arrested from a hooch den. . .

A girl child is subjected to a greater degree of exploitation. In a male-dominated society she is considered a burden to the family. The prevalence of dowry system makes her position more vulnerable. Even in the 21st century, her right to receive education is denied in many homes. Female literacy rate stands at a meager 54% while the sex ratio is 933 women per 1000 men.[30] Pre-birth elimination of the female child and female infanticide are rampantly resorted to in many regions of India. This has led to the imbalance in sex-ratio. Another hazard a girl child is forced to suffer is early marriage. This often has the effect of devastating her, physically and psychologically. Early marriage at times lands her in prostitution also.[31]

As regards female infanticide the state of Madhya Pradesh has arguably taken the lead over other states:[32]

> And usually they also decide to abort the child, should it be female. Often the women go through the process without seeking any help from their menfolk. Victims of a patriarchal society, their sensitivities have been so conditioned so as to make them easily adjust to such painful situations, remorse

30. *Census of India*, 2001; Also see S. Wadhwa's article in *Outlook*, July 12, 2004.
31. *The Times of India*, Kolkata, August 9, 2004.
32. Vinati Bhargava has elaborately discussed the state of female infanticide in Madhya Pradesh — See *The Statesman*, Siliguri, December 14, 2004.

> being little or zero. Such is the pressure that women have sometimes killed their new-born baby girls. . .
>
> . . .The birth of girls has traditionally never been celebrated among Gujjars, Rajputs and Yadavas, the dominant communities in Bhind and Morena (Madhya Pradesh) . . .
>
> . . .Demand for huge dowries, physical insecurity of women in a violence-prone region, the two-child norm and the socio-economic set-up where a male child is seen as the pillar of support or the link that ensures the continuance of family lineage are some reasons why a girl child is undesirable.

Foetal sex determination through ultrasound clinics has further aggravated the situation. Although illegal, there has been a mushroom growth of such clinics in rural Madhya Pradesh.

The reports on female foeticide in the city of Patiala were also harrowing. Patiala Police in August 2006 unearthed 25 foetuses from a well near a sex determination clinic. The foetuses were three to five months old.[33]

We can also reiterate that abuse perpetrated against the girl children is not attributable to poverty alone. Instead, a complex social psyche composed of a variety of ingredients like dowry system, social insecurity of women, overwhelming male dominance as an expression of feudal characteristics of the society, rampant illiteracy besides poverty can be held responsible for female infanticide and numerous other atrocities commited against the minor girls.

It is customary to blame the people of the rural districts of India for discrimination against minor girls. But recent census figures have laid bare the fact that India's sex ratio is worse in cities than in rural regions.[34]

---

33. *The Times of India*, Kolkata, August 12, 2006.
34. *The Times of India*, Kolkata, September 13, 2004.

The child sex ratio, concerning the population under the age of 6, shows greater disproportion between males and females.

> The Jainas are the only community in which the urban figure exceeds the rural and that by the narrowest of margins. The urban members pick up a little and the rural ones fall a bit. Again the trend holds across most states and communities with even fewer exceptions. . . . The only state in which matters look distinctly better in the 0-6 age group is Tamil Nadu, where urban child sex ratios are better than rural ones for each of the three major religious groups — Hindus, Muslims and Christians.
>
> So what explains this apparently perverse relationship between "development" and gender equality? Perhaps it is because the towns afford better access to sex determination tests. The fact that girl children in the village are put to work at an early age may also have something to do with it.

It is reasonable to infer that urbanization and gender equality do not go hand in hand in India. The problems of child abuse as well as gender inequality are multifaceted as we have so far discussed. As they are inextricably interwoven, any step to compartmentalize them will be futile and efforts intended to solve these problems should take into consideration various factors behind them.

4

The Children in Conflict with the Law

> But ill he lived, much evil saw
> With men to whom no better law
> Nor better life was known
> Deliberately and undeceived
> Those wild men's vices he received,
> And gave them back his own.
>
> — **Wordsworth**

Under the *Juvenile Justice Act* 1986, children below 16 years were classified as juveniles. But an amendment of the Act in 2000 has raised the age limit to 17 years. Despite that there was some confusion about the definition of the term in criminal jurisprudence. In 2005, the apex court of India, putting an end to the confusion, ruled that the date of committing an offence would determine whether an accused is entitled to the benefit of the *Juvenile Justice Act*.[1]

So a child below 18 years of age, accused of penal offence is tried under the *Juvenile Justice Act*. He is supposed to stay in a reformatory home instead of an ordinary jail. As per provisions of the *JJA* he is to be treated leniently. The apex court also ruled that the children tried as ordinary criminals for crimes committed by them, when they were between

1. See for details *The Times of India*, Kolkata, February 3, 2005.

sixteen and eighteen years of age at the time of promulgation of the Act (*JJA 2000*), would be reverted to juvenile courts.[2]

Interestingly, the expression *juvenile delinquent* has of late been replaced by *child in conflict with the law*, a euphemism popular with the modern social activists. We have no reason to discard the application of the new phrase but the high incidence of serious crimes, perpetrated by minors in India in recent times, prompts us to consider the phrase as an understatement. No wonder that children falling prey to hostile socio-economic environment turn into delinquents. Poverty in this respect plays a major part. But there are children whose proclivity to criminal activities is genetically determined. The Indian *children in conflict with the law* comprise both the types — the ordinary offenders, usually victims of poverty, and the genetically-prompted ones.

For the latter, the borstals or the reformatory homes cannot essentially be very useful. Researches in genetics may in future provide a solution to their problems. Although in the present dissertation we are concerned with the former class of the *children in conflict with the law* we cannot afford to overlook the latter since the domain of juvenile delinquency accommodates both the classes existing almost inseparably. Here is a perfect example of this mix-up. In January 2005, an eight-year-old girl was murdered by some children, a little

---

2. Ibid.

Earlier the Supreme Court had held that irrespective of the age of the juvenile at the time of offence, the Act would be applicable only if he was below 18 years at the time when he was produced in the court for the first time. But a five judge bench of the Supreme Court comprising justices N. Santosh Hegde, S.N. Variava, B.P. Singh, H.K. Sema and S.B. Sinha overruled the earlier judgement.

older than her, at a desolate place in the Murshidabad district of West Bengal:[3]

> Six boys aged between 10 and 14 were arrested last night for killing Rupa Haldar, an eight-year-old girl whose mutilated body was found in a mustard field. . . .
>
> . . .Ashique Haldar, Milan Das, Feroze Sheikh, Jayanta Haldar, Utpal Pal and Rajesh Haldar murdered Rupa at Hariharpara, 230 KM from Kolkata, because she saw them stealing vegetables. Rajesh is a student of class III and Jayanta and Utpal of class II. Feroze in class VII of a local high school, while Ashique and Milan are drop-outs.
>
> Rupa had been missing since she left home after returning from school on January 15. She was found buried in a shallow grave in the mustard field two days later.

The boys were arrested soon after and during interrogation by the police they gave a graphic description of how they killed the little girl. On that fateful afternoon Rupa saw the boys plucking vegetables. She told them that she would inform the owner of the crops about the theft. Consequently the boys became very angry and chased her. As she was held by them. Ashique throttled her to death. Then all the boys made a concerted effort in hiding the victims's body under a culvert, a little away from the scene of the crime. The following night they dragged the body to a nearby mustard field and buried her in a shallow grave.[4]

Worth noticing are some important aspects of the crime. (a) It was a cold-blooded murder committed by some children on their own. (b) Ashique and Milan were school drop-outs

---

3. *The Telegraph*, Kolkata, January 26, 2005.
4. Ibid.

who would very often drink alcohol and smoke *ganja* (a drug prepared from cannabis). They were mentors to the other boys. Ashique throttled the girl to death and confessed that he along with his friends brutalised the body of the victim with knives. (c) The murder had nothing to do with poverty or economic distress of either the victim or the murderers.

The gory details of the crime, particularly the way the body of the victim was brutalised lead us to hold that some of the murderers had a genetic proclivity to commit such crimes. Ashique, the principal accused who throttled the girl to death was possibly a classic example. The above case also demonstrated how children with natural tendency to perpetrate crime can influence many others.

Many more cases illustrate the fact that poverty is not essentially the root cause of all crimes committed by juveniles. In January 2003, many Kolkata dailies reported a robbery committed in the city with which a boy aged about 16 years was closely involved. Son of a reputed physician couple he was a student of a well-known public school of south Kolkata. His propensity to crime was attributed to loneliness and resultant frustration. His parents, quite affluent and well-placed, had to stay away from home for hours every day. They could take little care of the child. Driven by loneliness he developed close links with a gang of professional criminals and induced them to rob his neighbour with whom he had very cordial relations.[5] This is a demonstration of how uncared for and wayward children of affluent families take to crime.

School drop-outs, as is widely known, often indulge in criminal activities. The Murshidabad murder was an example

---

5. The case was reported in many dailies eg. *The Telegraph, The Anandabazar Patrika.*

where two school drop-outs, namely Ashique and Milan were the principal accused. In fact such instances galore. In October 2003 abduction of a trader in West Bengal caused sensation. Investigation revealed a school drop-out was involved with the crime.[6] Another illustration would not be out of place here:

> Rahul Halder was kidnapped on February 14. The class VIII student of Julien Day school in Kalyani, Nadia, was found last night by an RPF[7] sub-inspector at Titlagarh railway station in Orissa's Bolangir district.
>
> But Rahul's abduction was no run-of-the mill stuff. There was no ransom sought or paid.
>
> The kidnapper, Rahul's own classmate Niranjan Bagchi, wanted to teach him a lesson for having reported to the school principal that he had been reading pornography during class hours. At least that is what Rahul told Sub-Inspector G.P. Lenka before boarding a train for Kolkata with his father.
>
> Niranjan who stopped coming to school ever since the principal had initiated disciplinary action against him, waylaid me with four other boys on February 14 at a lonely spot some distance from my home and forced me into a waiting car. Niranjan said he would teach me a lesson for reporting against him. When I tried to shout for help, Niranjan and his gang gagged me and drove to a big railway station where they put me up on a departing train. One of the boys who had been driving the car was definitely above 20 years in age.[8]

---

6. *The Times of India*, Kolkata, October 19, 2004.
7. Railway Protection Force.
8. *The Hindustan Times*, Kolkata, February 18, 2005.

Niranjan had proven link with criminals. Otherwise it would not have been possible for him to plot the abduction of Rahul. Such nexus between school drop-outs and criminals is commonplace as evidenced by some cases described heretofore. No wonder that adolescent child workers also are naturally drawn to such nexus. Adolescents have a natural tendency to develop intimacy with the children of their own age group. The cameraderie generated in the process often provide the backdrop of some crimes perpetrated by juveniles. An interesting case reported from New Delhi supports our conjecture:[9]

> Three persons, including a juvenile, have been arrested from Mongolpuri in North West Delhi for kidnapping a four-year-old and asking for a ransom of Rs. 5 lakh for his release. One of the accused is a minor.
>
> Another accused, Gulshan, is a cousin of the boy. The boy's father. . .had complained to the police that his son had been kidnapped from near his house in Mongolpuri.
>
> Gulshan and his juvenile friend, who studies in class XII in a Rohini school, later told the police that they wanted the money to open a cyber cafe.

Next we come to a few more cases which will particularly interest the criminologists as well as the child rights activists.

To begin with mention may be made of a certain Bhola alias *HathKata* Bhola, a dreaded and well-known criminal aged about 16, who was killed by his rival gang at Jagaddal, a small industrial town in North 24 Parganas district of West Bengal. From early childhood, Bhola's propensity to criminal activities was manifest. In all likelihood, his behaviour pattern was

9. *The Times of India*, Kolkata, January 12, 2005.

genetically determined. He was instrumental in many cases of arson, burglary, riot, robbery and rape. Even at 12 he was known as a notorious criminal.[10]

Heinous crimes committed by juveniles are not exactly rare. Rape of a minor girl by a school drop-out named Rahul on the terrace of *Khuni Darwaja*, a medieval monument of Delhi on the Bahadurshah Zafar Marg, caused sensation in 2003. Rahul and his accomplice Amit were sentenced to life imprisonment. Rahul, wanted for burglary, was also convicted by the court under the *Arms Act* as he used a butcher's knife to immobilise the victim.[11] Rahul was a professional criminal who had just become a major in early 2003. But his reputation as a criminal was built much before he was convicted as an adult offender.

In recent times many more crimes of similar nature have been reported from different parts of the county:

> A teenager was raped, strangled and stuffed into a gunny bag before being thrown into a river by her boyfriend and his friends at Falta in South 24 Parganas. . . .
>
> Local residents spotted a gunny bag floating near the riverbank . . . on opening the sack they found the girl's body. The angry villagers beat up the girl's boyfriends and two of his friends, all in their teens, before handing them over to the police.
>
> On Saturday evening, the victim's boy friend called the girl out of her house at Nainan in Falta. Though it was a little late, her parents did not object as they had known the youth for long and also that they liked each other.[12]

---

10. *The Hindustan Times*, Kolkata, November 24, 2004.
11. *The Times of India*, Kolkata, January 18, 2005.
12. *The Hindustan Times*, March 28, 2005.

In another case reported from Karimpur (dist. Nadia, West Bengal), a fourteen-year-old boy raped a twelve-year-old girl known to him for a long time.[13] In both the cases the principal accused had no criminal records. It would however be simplistic to label such crimes as manifestations of value erosion leading to conflict with the law. These are actually crimes committed by adolescents with a criminal psyche, more often than not incorrigible.

Extreme covetousness, presumably a genetic trait found in some children, induce them to commit serious crimes. Chhat Falimari village near Basirhat (Coochbehar district), West Bengal, was the scene of one such crime in February, 2005. A two-year-old girl named Sushmita Das was thrown into a river by her neighbour Felani Das, a ten-year-old girl. Felani coveted the silver chain and anklet worn by the little girl. On the pretext of taking the girl for a stroll, Felani went to the riverside and threw her into the river. When the girl's parents asked her whereabouts later, Felani blatantly lied and told them that she had "escorted her back to the gate of her house."[14]

We should take notice of certain aspects of the case. Felani lost her father at a very early age and she had seven brothers and sisters. Abysmal poverty prevented her from attending school. No wonder she suffered from feelings of insecurity and deprivation which made her greedy. But it was quite uncanny that she threw the little girl into the river after taking possession of her ornaments knowing well that this would lead to her death. It was all the more astonishing since Felani was a close acquintance of the girl. So considering Felani's

---

13. *The Anandabazar Patrika,* February 10, 2005.
14. *The Anandabazar Patrika,* February 9, 2005.

age and circumstances it can be inferred that her behaviour was genetically determined.

Produced at the Coochbehar juvenile court Felani confessed that it was her greed for Sushmita's anklets that she threw the little girl into the river.

The types of crime children are usually involved with can be attributed to socio-economic environment. Low pay and appalling working conditions, unemployment and abuse often prompt child labourers to commit crime. Children working as domestic helps, waiters in restaurants and shop assistants sometimes work as informers of criminal gangs.

A recent case of theft reported from Hyderabad is worth describing. A 15-year-old girl had done it almost singlehandedly:[15]

> A maid decamped with gold ornaments and diamond jewellery all worth Rs. 7 lakhs from the house of retired army captain Waheed at Santosh Nagar colony in Asifnagar.
>
> According to a complaint lodged with the police, Shaheen (15) of Gooty in Anantapur district was working in the house of Waheed for the past 18 months. It was stated that the girl opened the iron safe and took away all the gold ornaments while Waheed's wife was fast asleep.

Very probably it was the first serious crime committed by the young girl. The opulent atmosphere of her employer's home was possibly an allure she could hardly resist and she coveted their wealth. But the carefully-woven plan indicated her crafty nature if there was no mastermind behind it. She escaped with the stolen articles when the watchman had gone into the house after being told that he was summoned by the houseowner for some other work.

---

15. *The New Indian Express* (Hyderabad), November 2, 2004.

One more case of a maid's involvement with a serious crime reported from Kolkata deserves mention. A girl working as a domestic help in a middle class home at Survey Park in Kolkata was arrested for abducting a child of her employer.[16] Her links with professional criminals were also revealed soon after.

As a matter of fact in most of such cases the delinquent maids were induced by professional criminals to commit such crime.

Far more intriguing was the case of a boy informer of Madhyamgram (Dist. North 24 Parganas), West Bengal. He was on the pay-roll of criminals. The boy would loiter in front of the counters of different banks and watch the customers withdrawing money. Next he would follow one of the customers to his home surreptitiously and pass on information about the address and other details of the customer to a professional gang of burglars. The house would be burgled soon after.[17]

No less dangerous are the juvenile muggers who target old and infirm people, women and children. A lone morning walker in a desolate place can easily fall prey to such juvenile delinquents. The Esplanade in Kolkata, Marine Drive and Juhu of Mumbai, Meharauli in Delhi are the places known for such activities.[18]

Bootlegging and smuggling seem to be among the professions most attractive to the juveniles with a propensity to crime. Delhi, Kolkata, Mumbai, Lucknow, Hyderabad and Guwahati are the cities where we come across numerous child

---

16. *The Anandabazar Patrika*, November 19, 2004.
17. *The Anandabazar Patrika*, August 2, 2004.
18. Bhattacharyya, M. S. *Bharate Sishusram*, pp. 71 ff, Kolkata, 2005.

drug peddlers, bootleggers and pimps. On the Indo-Nepal and Indo-Bangladesh borders smuggling is rampant and minors play a major role in these activities. Foreign clothes, watches, a variety of electronic gadgets, gold, cannabis, heroin, opium and even arms and ammunitions are smuggled through the borders. Children often carry headloads of smuggled goods across the border.

In northern Bengal, Assam and Bihar thousands of children are engaged in smuggling. In these regions they are known as *carriers.* Many of them are drug addicts. Particularly the bootleggers and drug peddlers are of a violent nature and often brawl in public places near the border.[19]

Some children in India get involved with burglaries in train compartments. They board a train in the guise of pedlars and procure information about passengers carrying valuables. The adult members of their gang, usually armed with lethal weapons rob the passengers of their belongings at an hour convenient to them.[20] Theft in railway compartments is a job somewhat easy for the juveniles because they seldom arouse suspicion.

Picking pockets is also among the professions most popular with the delinquent children of urban India. A child taking up this profession is rigorously trained after recruitment. Crowded trains and buses, shopping malls, busy thoroughfares, *ghats*, stadiums and theatres are their happy hunting ground. In this profession two or more children usually work together. While one picks the pocket the other children

---

19. Ibid. pp. 72 ff.

    In the Indo-Nepal and Indo-Bangladesh borders, I have witnessed their activities a number of times. Raising of the barbed wire fence along the Indo-Bangla border has reduced their activities to a degree.

20. M.S. Bhattacharyya, op. cit, p. 74.

carry away the booty in turn. The pickpockets are seldom caught red-handed and nearly in all cases hoodwink people and police alike.[21]

Also rampant are the cases of snatching in larger Indian towns and involvement of delinquent children with them is commonplace. Some cases are particularly interesting as they demonstrate tact, intelligence and leadership quality of the delinquent boys.

Sometimes the way they operate is quite amazing. In one such case of snatching, a man carrying some money in a bag was targeted by four boys aged between 11 and 16. One of them stealthily smeared mud on his shirt and went away. Another boy, walking by his side, told him about the dirty patches on his shirt and volunteered to help him cleaning it. The third member of the team then appeared on the scene with a pot of water and behaved as if he had no link with the other boys. One of them at this stage offered to hold the bag in which the money was kept. The victim, totally ignorant of the plot, asked one of them to hold the bag and started cleaning his shirt. At that moment the other boy snatched it from his hand and ran away. The man chased him for a while but lost him in the narrow and crowded street.[22]

Similar is the technique of cell phone snatchers of big cities like Kolkata and Mumbai:[23]

> Bijoy Kumar is 12, young enough not to arouse suspicions when he chatted up a target.

---

21. Ibid., p. 72.
22. Ibid., p. 73.
    In fact police officials in India come across many such cases every year.
23. *The Hindustan Times*, December 24, 2004.

> Samran Mahato is 14, barely noticeable in the crowd at a shopping mall or railway station.
>
> Once Bijay had struck a conversation, Samran would rush to the target, snatch his mobile phone and vanish into the crowd. And all the while, Ganga Mahato would keep an eye on the proceedings, ready to sound the alarm if there was any hint of danger.
>
> The police have nabbed the two boys and Ganga (22), but suspect other boys are involved in the racket.
>
> The arrested boys are from Sahebgunge village (Sic) in Jharkhand. They would catch a train from Tinpahar station to Howrah and put up in a hotel, remaining in the city till they had collected enough cells — say 50 or so.
>
> To them each was worth Rs. 500. The boys counted this amount as a fortune, while the price also suited dealers who could sell phones cheap and still make a big profit.
>
> Some of the cells reached dealers in the city, the boys would carry the rest back to Jharkhand. Once the bulk has been sold they would return to the city for another round. The police estimated that they stole and sold 1000 cell phones before they were caught.

It was in December 2004, that Kolkata police, spotted a young member of the gang aged about 12 with a cell phone. As he was very young and had an impoverished look, unbecoming of a cell phone user, police arrested him. Subsequently, he led them to the hotel in central Kolkata where Samran and Ganga were arrested and 22 cell phones were seized. It was also revealed that the malls and stations in south and central Kolkata, particularly the crowded ones, were the places where they prefer to operate. The gang operates in Mumbai and Lucknow besides Kolkata.

Interestingly, a part of the booty is exported to the neighbouring countries. The expensive cell phones have a ready market in foreign countries as well.[24]

Equally interesting was another case of snatching reported from Kolkata. Two young boys aged about twelve years were the offenders. One of them engaged a gentleman in conversation, the moment he came out of a bank with some money on his person. As he was distracted by the conversation, the other boy snatched the money away. As the police arrested them soon after, it was learnt that earlier they had committed similar crimes a number of times, learning the tricks from an older boy.[25]

In a consumerist society, juveniles are also drawn into conflict with the law owing to emotional problems. Such problems may assume serious dimensions:[26]

> Anamika Malakar, a teenager, was arrested today for allegedly hiring goons to kill a man who spurned her. Debashis Sarkar, 30, was called out of a hall where his wedding reception was being held on Sunday night by unknown youths and hacked to death. Police said the murder in Katwa, Burdwan, 150 Kms. from Kolkata, was an act of vengeance after Sarkar rejected the school girl's marriage proposal. She engaged assassins (sic) to kill him said a Katwa police station officer.

Violent anger of the ditched girl had led to this crime. In all likehood, she had no criminal bent of mind, genetically or otherwise.

---

24. *The Anandabazar Patrika*, December 29, 2004.
25. *The Anandabazar Patrika*, March 23, 2005.
26. *The Telegraph*, January 26, 2005.

There are other crimes committed by minors which most people would seek to downplay as trifles.

> A 13-year-old girl who went missing from Salt Lake on February 25, had been traced to Burdwan. Rimi Saha, a class VII student. . .did not return home from school. Her parents lodged a case of kidnapping at Bidhannagar police station.
>
> The police began investigations and found out that the girl, a resident of Keshtopur in North 24-Parganas, was having an affair with the driver of her school bus Sanjay Raut (22) and that Rimi had eloped with him.[27]

The drama however, didn't last long. Police officials, acting on a tip-off raided Sanjay's home and rescued Rimi. Meanwhile, Rimi had got married. Since child marriage was banned Sanjay was arrested by the police.[28] About the same time a similar case of 'kidnapping' was reported from Suburban Kolkata.

> Supriya Roy returned home on Sunday night. The police questioned her and took her into custody the moment they realized that she had staged her own kidnapping.
>
> . . .The police also arrested Bikash Bala and Badal Roy, with whom Supriya Roy had run away. There was no ransom involved. Bikash and Supriya simply wanted some hours of privacy. . .
>
> There is another charge against Supriya. She is an illegal migrant from Bangladesh. After crossing the border, Supriya and her brother Saikat lived at Barasat with an aunt, who's an Indian. The police are probing how she got admission to an Indian School.

---

27. *The Hindustan Times,* March 2, 2005.
28. Ibid.

An interesting case of fake abduction was reported from Baruipur in South 24 Parganas district of West Bengal in early March 2005. A boy aged about 14, a student of class IX had fled home as he wanted to skip his annual examinations. Fleeing home he rang up his father and told that he was abducted by a criminal gang who demanded a ransom. His efforts ended in a fiasco as he was nabbed by the police.[29] These incidents do not usually affect the common people. So they are not regarded as serious crimes. All the same they are instances of deviation from normal behaviour.

We have focused our attention on all three major factors responsible for crimes committed by the juveniles. These are economic, social and genetical. A bad environment, coupled with poverty and frustration may draw a child into a life of crime. When a child worker is thrown out of employment and fails to find a new job he becomes prone to criminal activities. The expansive world of the children in conflict with the law welcomes him where he associates with genetically motivated juvenile delinquents of various descriptions including the dreaded homicidal maniacs, besides the other types who are drifted into the world of crime by poverty and earn livelihood by mugging, picking pocket, snatching, passing on information to criminal gangs and perpetrating numerous other petty crimes.

---

29. *The Hindustan Times,* February 8, 2005.

5

Conclusion

THE problem of child labour and child abuse has assumed global dimensions. Any remedy for them therefore needs to be globally accepted. We have already discussed how Bangaladesh, Pakistan, Nepal and Bhutan have formed part of the area of operation of the child traffickers.[1] It is heartening to note that the SAARC countries have already expressed serious concern over the issue of child abuse. As early as 1988, at a conference on working children held in Kathmandu, Nepal, the South Asian Association for Regional Co-operation (SAARC) was urged to eliminate the trans-border flesh trade particularly involving minor girls in South Asia.[2] The conference pointed out that the efforts to root out flesh trade should be part of a larger plan to mitigate the problems of child labour and child abuse. It was also recommended that the SAARC countries undertake a special rehabilitation programme for minor children who had been forced into prostitution.

Nepal, during the same period, introduced stringent regulations and penalty for trafficking in women and female minors. Anyone caught after a sexual transaction involving a minor could merit a sentence of upto 20 years in prison.[3]

---

1. See for details — *The Times of India,* Kolkata, September 18, 2004.
2. *The Kuensel,* December 17, 1988.
3. Ibid.

In Bhutan, abject poverty in rural areas rendered it easy for the traffickers to bait their targets with promises of a lucrative job:[4]

> Low-caste girls, born with no hope for comfort, are particularly vulnerable. Such targets are usually approached when they are alone at home. . . The dream merchant pictures the luxuries of city life which the girl can have for herself if she takes the job with an attractive salary.
>
> Once an agreement is worked out, the girl is slipped out of the village, usually at night. While awaiting for (sic) an opportune time to get the girls across the border, a procurer may get some of them temporary employment in carpet weaving or garment making. A trafficker gets about US $1000 for each girl who reaches a particular destination.

The foregoing report was published in *Kuensel* (Bhutan's national newspaper) way back in 1988. The SAARC conference held in Kathmandu that year was seen as a major landmark in the fight against child labour and child abuse. Unfortunately hopes were too high while the achievements minimal. Reviewed after a lapse of sixteen years, the chinks and crevices of our policies have become apparent. Lack of political will and a considerable degree of indifference on the part of the officials entrusted with the task of implementing the policies were crucially important factors. Trans-border trafficking in children could have been checked through restrictions on movement of minor children from the economically backward regions of Nepal, Bhutan and Bangladesh to India. Indian towns like Siliguri, because of their geographical proximity with the countries mentioned above have become safe haven for the traffickers. The U.N., the UNICEF or the SAARC should

4. Ibid.

have appointed monitors in these towns to watch independently the influx of children into these towns and apprise the local authorities of such trans-border movements. Interestingly, *Maiti Nepal,* an organization based in Nepal has exactly done this in 2004. It has decided to launch its movement against trafficking of Nepali girls in Siliguri also as the town has always been the "locale of rampant trafficking." A sister organization of *Maiti Nepal,* namely *Kanchanjungha Uddhar Kendra* (Kanchanjungha Rescue Centre) was formed in Siliguri in December 2004. The organization and its current chairperson Mrs Anuradha Koirala did a commendable job:[5]

> Mrs Koirala said that with the support of *Kanchanjungha Uddhar Kendra,* it would conduct social awareness campaigns against girl trafficking from the community level to the national level in the country. These campaigns would include discussions, interaction, and workshops. . . These campaigns have been effective in seeking public support, creating social pressure and advocacy against girl trafficking in Nepal, Mumbai and Delhi. . . It would also conduct awareness and income-generating skill training-programmes for girls. . .
>
> The *Maiti Nepal* has formed a number of transit homes along the Indo-Nepalese border to intercept trafficked girls, before they could be taken across the border, and return them safely to their homes.
>
> The organization has also conducted a monitoring campaign at the main entry points along the border to confirm the rate of trafficking here.

---

5. *The Statesman,* Siliguri, December 13, 2004.

> She said that every year some 6000 to 7000 Nepalese girls of six to fourteen years, are being trafficked and sold to brothels in several parts of the country.
>
> In most of the cases they have fallen prey to several diseases, fatal of them being the AIDS. She said that most of these girls are from economically backward families and they are sold to brothels of Mumbai, Pune, Kolkata and Siliguri.
>
> Mrs Koirala felt that imposition of visa on the Indo-Nepalese border would help in reducing the rate of trafficking from Nepal. "Open border is one of the major reasons behind the rampant trafficking," she said.
>
> She further said that police and custom officers of both countries hardly help in checking the rate of trafficking owing to their vested interests.
>
> According to Mrs Koirala, Kakarvita and Pashupatinagar are the two places along the border of Nepal, from where girls are trafficked to India the most.

The most important point the chairperson of *Maiti Nepal* emphasized was "the need of sensitizing the government machinery and police administration" to the dangers of trafficking and also to developing the socio-economic scenario of the region.[6]

A report published in the *Times of India* (Kolkata) on September 18, 2004, corroborates[7] the findings of *Maiti Nepal.*

This is however one part of the story of internationalization of child abuse which concerns India's

---

6. Ibid.
7. The *TOI* report mentioned the plight of the minor girls trafficked from Bangladesh also along with those from Nepal and Bhutan.

northern and north-eastern borders. We have in store still more surprising parts of the story.

In January 2005, the UNICEF confirmed a case of trafficking in children orphaned by the tsunami disaster.[8]

> Reports of children being taken away surfaced soon after the killer waves swamped 13 nations, killing more than 1,53,000 people and leaving more than a million people injured and homeless. But the UNICEF report is the first confirmed case.
>
> The International Organization for Migration (IOM) also said today that an Indonesian aid agency had reported seven cases of child trafficking since the December 26 undersea earthquake that sent giant waves crashing ashore across Asia and East Africa.
>
> Birgithe Lund-Henriksen, chief of the UNICEF in Indonesia child protection unit, said UNICEF and Indonesian police had confirmed that a four-year-old boy was taken out of Banda Aceh, the capital of devastated Aceh province, by a couple claiming to be his parents.
>
> Local police were alerted after non-governmental organizations (NGOs) became suspicious when the couple took the child to a hospital in Medan, 450 kms. south-east of Banda Aceh, she said.
>
> "NGOs grew suspicious when the couple were not consistent in their story," she said, adding they now say they are the boy's neighbours.

This case can be likened to the case of fake adoption of a minor girl named Payel[9] in Bandel, (WB) India, mentioned

8. *The Telegraph*, Kolkata, January 8, 2005.
9. *The Anandabazar Patrika*, December 17, 2004.

earlier. Abusers, irrespective of their places of origin, often adopt similar techniques. There ought to be global characteristics of a global problem. What distinguishes the Banda Aceh case from the Bandel case is the active and expeditious intervention of the UNICEF and the local NGOs in the former. Such actions should be more wide-ranging, forming part of a comprehensive action plan.

Curiously enough some of the orphaned victims of the tsunami disaster were to be trafficked into India through the Kolkata port:[10]

> That child traffickers have chosen Kolkata as their transit point for selling off tsunami orphans from Sri Lanka is no coincidence. It is the city's unusually low conviction rate of traffickers that has encouraged the gang.
>
> . . . Coast guard officials said that a special alert has been issued following reports that a fishing vessel carrying tsunami orphans is on its way from Colombo to the shores of Kolkata.
>
> The trawler set sail in the first week of January and is scheduled to reach any day.
>
> . . .It is feared that the orphans could be sold as sex slaves or as bonded labourers. A similar warning has come from UNICEF after it received reports of criminals offering kidnapped children from Aceh in Indonesia for sale. "We have also got reports of a text message advertising an auction of about 300 orphans" a UNICEF official said.
>
> Many of the child traffickers could the posing as aid workers or family friends. The aim is to stop gangs from whisking

10. *The Hindustan Times*, January 20, 2005.

> away orphaned children into trafficking networks, before selling them into forced labour or sexual slavery in wealthier countries such as Malaysia and Singapore. "I am sure it's happening. So the law-enforcing agencies should take utmost care in nabbing the entire gang," the official said.

The cases mentioned hereinbefore vouch for the claim that child abuse is a global issue. Next we take up for discussion the problem of rehabilitation of the child workers, the children in conflict with the law and the victims of abuse. We will confine our observations to India.

Strange notions float about that the best way to rehabilitate the abused children is to send them back to their parents. It has often backfired to the dismay of social activists.

Earlier we have cited a good many examples of child abuse by parents of which the most awful was the case of Bhirana Devi of Hajipur, Bihar, who sold off her infant son for Rs. 6000.[11] Such parents are in fact victims of the same socio-economic milieu which is responsible for perpetuation of child labour, child abuse and juvenile delinquency. Neither their mindset nor the environment will change overnight. We have instances of parents refusing to take back their abused children to their homes. The case of Guriya, an eight-year-old girl from the suburbs of Kolkata was sensational.[12] She was mauled by a pet dog kept at her employer's house which was locked from outside. The young domestic help was rescued by the neighbours who had to break in and rush her to hospital in a severely injured condition. She was discharged from hospital after her recovery and taken to a police station since her mother, a single parent, refused to take her back.[13]

---

11. *The Statesman*, Kolkata, September 14, 2004.
12. *The Times of India*, Kolkata, March 12, 2005.
13. Ibid.

At times abused children themselves refuse to go back to their homes. This is exactly what happened in the case Dipika, a school girl from Orissa, who left home on her own, unable to tolerate "the regular physical and mental torture" by her father.[14] More rebellious was the attitude of some tribal girls of Chattisgarh campaigning against child marriage.[15]

> Call them rebellious, but these children have a lesson or two for their parents. Over 1000 minor girls in this district (Rajnadgaon) of Chhattisgarh have turned against their elders, saying they are too young to be married off.
>
> A class VII student, now heads a band of girls who scamper around getting signatures for a petition against child marriages. And they acted just in time, days ahead of *teej* festival, when dozens — often hundreds — of girls barely into puberty are dragged to the altar by their parents.

Such resistance from the children against the dictates of their parents was the ray of hope for millions of minor girls in India, particularly in the states of Rajasthan, Madhya Pradesh, Bihar, UP, Jharkhand; Haryana, Chhattishgarh and Andhra Pradesh where prevalence of child marriage is a chronic problem and the role played by parents in such marriages is deplorable.

If alone, a girl cannot assert her rights in the face of overwhelming odds. Very recently a tribal girl from Keonjhar (Orissa) had to flee her home[16] and take refuge in a forest for quite a few days, to avoid early marriage. Minati, the 13-year-old was to be married to a 50-year-old man.

---

14. *The Hindustan Times*, Kolkata, February 14, 2005.
15. *The Times of India*, Kolkata, April 23, 2005.
16. *The Anandabazar Patrika*, March 24, 2005.

The custom has nothing to do with poverty or per capita income. Gujarat, a comparatively prosperous state with a higher per capita income has a very high incidence of child marriage (1 in 45) while Orissa with a low per capita income has a low incidence (1 in 83).[17] In fact alertness on the part of the law enforcing authorities, stern legal action against the offenders and above all resistance against the custom by the minor girls themselves can bring about a change.[18]

While remaining steadfast to the principle that institutional care is the best way of rehabilitating rescued children and juvenile offenders we must also examine the condition of *juvenile homes* or *rescue homes,* usually run by the state governments in India. More often than not they are badly run and the child inmates detest them cordially.[19]

> Ten Children had been shifted from *Kisalay* (a Kolkata rescue home) to another home for destitute children for lack of space. A day later, 5 of them fled their new home — the conditions being too distressing and the meals inadequate.
>
> The five boys ran away from the *home* in Basirhat last Thursday. But, it was not until Sunday that the authorities informed the cops. The boys were among 10 inmates of the state-run *Kisalay* home in Barasat who were shifted to the shelter at Chhoto Jirakpur in Basirhat.

---

17. *The Times of India.* April 23, 2005.
18. The origin of the custom of child marriage can be traced back to the early medieval period, when foreign invaders frequently carried away even the minor girls along with the booty after they overran a town or a village. The common people, defenseless against such marauders, started marrying off their minor daughters in order to save them from disgrace — see for details. *The Times of India,* Kolkata, April 23, 2005.
19. *The Hindustan Times,* Kolkata, April 4, 2005.

> . . . When policemen went to the home on Sunday to investigate the case, the inmates had shocking tales on the distressing conditions that they live in. They also complained of meals that rarely filled their stomachs.

The condition of the *homes* was more or less the same in other states also. On March 18, 2005, some inmates of a *remand home* in Patna (Bihar) had escaped, exposing the callousness of the authorities and the distress they were subjected to, during their stay at the *home.*[20]

The *homes* meant for the girls have a different set of problems for the inmates. A recent report from Guntur, a city in Andhra Pradesh was an eye-opener. The inmates of a *home* in the town were mercilessly beaten up for informing some outsiders about their problems. They lived in a dilapidated building which badly needed electricity. Further, the warden, instead of staying with them, lived in her village which was away from the *home.* Some of the girls were forced to work at her village home for which they were never paid wages.[21]

In all these *homes*, where a saviour or for that matter, a guardian, metamorphoses into a tormentor, thorough reforms are an immediate necessity.

Most acute is the problem of rehabilitation of the children in conflict with the law. The case of a juvenile offender from Mumbai discussed earlier, is worth remembering.[22] He had no place to go after becoming a major. Similar was the case of some inmates of a Kolkata *home* who agitated against the decision of the authorities to expel them as they were no longer minors. One of them even tried to commit suicide when he

---

20. I am indebted to *NDTV*, a private TV channel for the information.
21. *The New Indian Express*, Hyderabad, November 2, 2004.
22. *The Times of India*, Kolkata, had reported this case on 12.10.04

heard that authorities had turned down their request for reconsideration of the decision.

The position of the child, once in conflict with the law, is forever precarious. In the *remand homes* he seldom learns anything worthwhile that can help him eke out a livelihood on his own. He is socially ostracized and therefore finds it hard to get even a job of an unskilled worker.

If a child is not a habitual offender genetically prone to crime, a little empathy for him can do marvels to restore him to normal life. We will now look to one such recent case reported from Mumbai:[23]

> This story began on May 17 last year when Shyam Yadav (name changed), a class X student from Thane's St. John the Baptist High School stabbed his mother to death in their flat and fled with Rs. 3000.

This was apparently a crude and bizarre manifestation of Oedipus complex. The boy reportedly had never demonstrated any vices and it seemed he committed the crime on the spur of the moment. He was repentant and required trauma counselling. The principal of his school sent one of his teachers to meet him. Interestingly, the teacher was impressed by his desire to lead a normal life. She continued with her counselling, casting aside all inhibitions about a crime like this. Soon after the boy was released on bail and went back home.[24] Such efforts by teachers and school authorities may lead to splendid achievements.

What enthused the social activists in India in recent times is the way some institutions and individuals are fighting

---

23. *The Times of India,* Kolkata, April 15, 2005.
24. Ibid.

against child labour and child abuse. Vociferous protests by some child rights groups have forced a private TV channel (MTV) to withdraw an advertisement for Pepsi which showed a child serving Pepsi soft drinks to the members of a cricket team. The protest movement was led by two Mumbai-based NGOs, namely *Balprafula* and *Yuva*. They took up the issue with Pepsi and eventually the advertisement was modified.[25]

What role dedicated teachers can play in combating child labour is evident in the Sraddha Bhawan schools in Orissa:[26]

> Three hundred and sixty eight tribal children have been withdrawn from the work force and are seen reading in the class rooms. It has happened in Keonjhar district, the place that recorded a steep rise in primary school drop-out rates a few years ago.
>
> A few unemployed local youths have made this dream come true in the tribal pockets of Keonjhar. Their successful motivation for the school drop-outs and the non-school going children has given birth to a new type of school named Sraddha Bhawan.
>
> Today Sraddha Bhawan, being run by the People's Cultural Centre (PECUC), in Patna Block of Keonjhar district has become a ray of hope for thousands of children, providing them joyful learning, preparatory education for the non-school going among them, and a bridge course for the drop-outs.
>
> The PECUC had identified that the hectic daily schedule of the schools and the uninteresting curriculum was largely

25. *The Times of India*, Kolkata, October 1, 2004.
26. See for details, Manjusri Reddy's feature in *Sahara Time*, New Delhi, November 20, 2004.

> responsible for the increase in drop-out rates in primary schools. Hence it was planned to make education more interesting through fun-pictures, stories, role play, puzzles, along with warm-up games, songs etc. The curriculum has been developed for the Shraddha Bhawan accordingly by experienced personnel from the District Primary Education Programme (DPEP) and other consultants in which education was made more interesting and palatable.

The region, inhabited mostly by tribals has a literacy rate as low as 30% according to 2001 census. Agriculture, collection of forest products and livestock rearing are the mainstay of the economy of the region. In order to supplement the meagre income of the people, children are engaged in agriculture, construction projects, animal husbandry, collection of forest products and domestic chores. They stop going to schools. So the drop-out rate in the tribal schools was more than 60 per cent.[27] But the Shraddha Bhawan brought about the transformation.

> The PECTUC has been running 10 such Shraddha Bhawans to bring drop-outs back to school in 10 villages in northern Keonjhar for the past four years. Today a total of 1162 tribal non-school going drop-outs and child labourers are enrolled in Shraddha Bhawans for preparatory education and bridge course.
>
> Fun school was not the only idea behind forming the Shraddha Bhawans. . .counselling of parents, employers, teachers and community as a whole, formation of mothers' self-help groups, working towards socio-economic empowerment of women, formation of *Sisu Mahasabha* at the village levels as a strategy for protecting child rights,

27. Ibid.

> health check-up and immunization and sensitisation and awareness campaign on the need and relevance of education and other aspects relating to child rights, all these formulated the ideal learning process. .
>
> . . .All the Shraddha Bhawan children are getting free treatment, medicines and regular check-ups. 476 children have been immunized against various communicable diseases, 319 children were identified with different diseases and have been treated. A *Sikhya Vikash Panthy*, a fund raising process, has also been initiated by the community with the encouragement of PECUC to sustain the efforts. In the first month, 189 households contributed about Rs. 1615 for this fund.
>
> Shraddha Bhawan, which has attracted more than 100 school drop-outs in such a short span now intends to ratify the fun-learning system throughout the state.[28]

The experience of Shraddha Bhawan is unique and can be shared through the length and breadth of India instead of Orissa alone. The most important features of this concept was the drawing up of an interesting curriculum for the children keeping in mind the need of various age groups, introduction of a bridge course for drop-outs to enable them to cope with other learners, medical facilities for the children and counselling for the parents.

A group of four tribal youths of Tripura, working independently, has come up with almost similar results. In a remote village named Paharkoutal they have established a hostel meant for the school drop-outs. This hostel called *Sandhuk Satra Tangthai* has brought back many young children to the residential school. Provided with barest essentials of

28. Ibid.

Ragpickers at work. (Courtesy: Ashish Mukherjee)

Slum children of Kolkata living in squalor.

The inevitable school drop-outs.
Children with their homeless parents.

Children queue up before distribution of refreshment
by an NGO. Bhutani island, Malda Dist., W.B.
(Courtesy: Soma Bhattacharya)

life like very simple food and lodging, the children happily go to school. The organizers of the school had taken into consideration the fact that free education alone cannot attract the children of the poverty-stricken tribal village to school.[29]

In April 2000, a survey conducted at Bhutni, an island in the river Ganga in West Bengal revealed that food offered to the hungry children in schools can reduce the drop-out rate significantly.[30]

What was considered a stray experiment in 2000 turned into a reality in 2005:[31]

> In an order that could attract more children to schools, the Supreme Court has fixed January 2005 as the deadline for all states to provide cooked meals to students upto class V as the centre had decided to provide an additional Re. 1 per child to meet cooking costs. "We direct that every child eligible for cooked meal under the mid-day meal scheme in all states and union territories, shall be provided with the said meal immediately and, in any case, not later than January 2005," a Bench of Mr. Justice Y.K. Sabharwal and Mr. Justice S.H. Kapadia ordered. The court dealing with a PIL filed by the People's Union for Civil Liberties made it clear that "it would not be open to the state governments or the union territories to delay the implementation of the

---

29. *The Anandabazar Patrika,* December 13, 2004.
30. Some school children in the island were provided with food and clothing between 2000 and 2004. Although not continuous, the distribution of food and school uniform generated much enthusiasm among the students and drop-out rate in those schools where food was distributed fell sharply compared to those where no such scheme was introduced. The survey was conducted by an NGO, namely Bhutni Youth Education Society.
31. *The Statesman,* Novemebr 25, 2004.

scheme beyond January 2005 on the ground that the necessary assistance had been released by the centre.

This was indeed an epoch-making decision. Within a few months after mid-day meals were first served, there had been considerable increase in attendance of students in schools. Moreover a multitude of children are seeking enrolment in schools while the school authorities find it extremely difficult to accommodate them because of inadequate infrastructural facilities. Most of the schools, particularly in the rural areas and slums of the big towns, have dilapidated buildings, with insufficient space for children.[32] In some villages there is no building at all for a school and the children have no other way but to attend open air classes.[33]

Lack of infrastructure therefore is a stumbling block to solving the problem of re-enrolment of school drop-outs in India.

One is tempted to suggest a few more measures nevertheless. The primary schools can be upgraded to class VI standard thereby accommodating almost all pre-teen children in the schools. The schools so upgraded can be classified as *general* and *rehab* schools, the latter meant for the huge number of drop-outs and abused children. But this will entail huge expenditure which the governments alone cannot defray. Here comes the issues of involving various NGOs which have shown keen interest in abolition of child labour

32. I have visited many such schools where the drop-out rates have come down and applications for fresh enrolments have piled up. Photographs of some dilapidated school buildings are printed in this book.

33. It happens more in flood-ravaged areas. Financial constraints is often the main reason for absence of infrastructure.

and individual and institutional donors in India and abroad eager to help the cause of the distressed children.

Now let us turn to some remarkable changes with regard to treatment of children in schools. Here also the court's intervention played a vital role. Earlier we have examined many instances of child abuse in schools. At long last, Kolkata High court in a landmark judgement expressed great displeasure with cases of child abuse in schools and instructed the government of West Bengal to take necessary steps in this respect. Consequently the directorate of school education in West Bengal issued a memorandum to all schools in West Bengal:[34]

> "Corporal punishment to students is not only useless, but is harmful to the mental growth of students apart from the fact that it may cause physical injury to the students. . .
>
> . . . Teachers, in general, have rejected corporal punishment. In spite of this, unfortunate instances, though very rare, sometimes occur when teachers are found to resort to corporal punishment. Such action on their part is very undesirable. . .
>
> . . .It is brought to the notice of all teachers in primary and secondary schools that caning or any other type of corporal punishment is strictly prohibited and if any teacher resorts to such type of punishment, it will be dealt with strictly.

We have already discussed how child abuse affect the relationship between the teachers and the students. Mutual hatred and mistrust cannot augur well for the future of the young learners. Indeed some teachers have attitudinal problems as their mind is gripped by obsolescent ideas.

---

34. *The Times of India,* Kolkata, August 17, 2004.

Children fail to cope with an age-old value system the teachers want them to adhere to because they have a different set of values and expectations. The conflict and the strained relationship resulting from it at times leads to violence. We have a recent example from a remote village where some young students aged between 13 and 15 set fire to their school building causing great damage to the record room of the school as they failed their annual exams. Earlier they had requested the school authorities to reconsider their decision to fail them which was turned down.[35] It may be of interest to note here that neither the school nor its teachers were known for their academic excellence. The righteous indignation of the students therefore, found expression in violence which undoubtedly was no solution to the problem. Apart from raising the level of knowledge of some teachers through training, there must be some efforts to make them a little more sensible. The association of teachers of the Anglo-Indian schools, subsequent to the suicide of a student of St. Joseph's convent Chandernagore in 2005, suggested some important measures. C. R. Gasper, the principal of St. Augustine's Day School and a member of the association pointed out:[36]

> Regular seminars, workshop and counselling should be organized by the schools to educate both teachers and parents in the changing problem of students. We need to be updated first to guide our adolescent children.

The association decided to organize counselling for teachers so that they can develop cordial relationship with the students.

---

35. See for details — *Anandabazar Patrika*, May 1, 2005. The school is situated at Mahadipur, a village in Malda district (West Bengal). I chanced to visit the school sometime ago and gathered first-hand information about it.

36. *The Telegraph*, April 8, 2005.

Such counselling is supposed to include discussions with teachers on adolescent problems. The president of the association unequivocally mentioned:[37]

> The students are our main concern. Schools are meant for them. Why shouldn't they feel secured to discuss their problems with teachers.

The change of attitude is encouraging and no doubt it will give relief to many school children.

Abuse of female child, infanticide and foeticide are among the other problems we have discussed earlier. The declining sex ratio has attracted the attention of the members of Indian parliament recently. The members of the Loka Sabha expressed concern over the issue and unanimously emphasized the need to change the attitude to the girl child so that socio-economic distortion could be avoided.[38]

Some state governments in India have also initiated vigorous campaigns to bring about a change in the attitude of people to the female child. The state of Andhra Pradesh, known for her not-too-good records in this respect has showed the way; so much so that the latest tennis icon of India Sania Mirza, a girl from Andhra Pradesh, is projected by the state as a role model. Worried about the poor sex ratio the state has announced an incentive of over Rs. 1 lakh to couples having single girl child.[39]

---

37. Ibid.
38. *The Times of India*, Kolkata, May 4, 2005.
39. *The Times of India*, Kolkata, March 15, 2005; In 2003, altogether 383 cases of child abuse was reported from Andhra Pradesh. This was the third largest figure reported. The first two places were occupied by Madhya Pradesh (699) and Maharashtra (605). — See for details. Nandini R. Iyer's report in *the Hindustan Times*, Kolkata, May 4, 2005.

These incidents indicate a significant departure from the earlier policies of the state governments in India. Evidently, there had been a paradigm shift emphasizing a holistic approach to the problems.

Hopefully, the change in attitude at different levels would herald a new era in which love and care will substitute oppression and abuse of children.

Index